This publication is an excellent addition to the research on the evangelical community already published by the EA. It is academically grounded, accessible and easy to read with a wealth of interesting, helpful and useful information for policymakers and Christian leaders.
Ram Gidoomal CBE, Chairman, Lausanne International Board, South Asian Concern and Traidcraft

When a number of surveys have taken place on either a similar subject or using the same sample of respondents, it is always good to evaluate not just each individual study but all the studies taken as a whole. That is what this book does and so gives a wider, larger overview of the group in question – in this case evangelicals on the database of the Evangelical Alliance ... This book very usefully looks in detail at key issues tangent on the church today – theological considerations, family and social life, gender, UK politics and worldwide issues – which can only help strategic reflection in deciding what actions should be taken to enhance church growth and the spread of the gospel.
Peter Brierley, Senior Lausanne Associate for Church Research

Evangelicals – like all Christians – are called to be in the world but not of it. The extensive data contained in the book will reveal how they set about this challenge, bearing in mind that they do not all do the same thing. In short, the detail matters and exists in abundance in these insightful essays, all of which repay very careful reading.
Grace Davie, Professor of Sociology, University of Exeter

Here is a thorough and thoughtful attempt to paint a picture of the evangelical world, its impact on and contribution to the wider church and society as a whole. The research produces many fascinating insights which will inform the way evangelicals understand themselves and their movement. It raises questions and concerns about trends and will therefore be a useful resource in fashioning the way the evangelical tradition develops for the future.
The Rt Revd Julian Henderson, Bishop of Blackb·····

G000244818

These reflections simplify the complexities inherent in surveys of this nature that cover different aspects of evangelical Christianity in the UK. Presenting a good blend of academic insights in easy-to-understand language, this book is an invaluable resource to pastors and gospel ministers in understanding the state of Christianity and ministry in the twenty-first-century United Kingdom.

Dr Daniel Akhazemea, Principal, Christ the Redeemer College and Chairman, RCCGUK National Advisory Board on Education and Training

As a local pastor-leader caught up with the daily challenges of the pastoral tasks, it is a privilege to read ... the latest objective survey on a whole spectrum of important subjects affecting society and church.

Pastor OSH, Senior Pastor, Chinese Church in London (CCiL)

21st Century Evangelicals

Reflections on Research by the Evangelical Alliance

Evangelical Alliance
edited by Greg Smith

instant
ap☐stle

First published in Great Britain in 2015

Instant Apostle
The Barn
1 Watford House Lane
Watford
Herts
WD17 1BJ

British Library Cataloguing-in-Publication Data

A catalogue record for this book is available from the British Library

This book and all other Instant Apostle books are available from Instant Apostle:

Website: www.instantapostle.com

E-mail: info@instantapostle.com

ISBN 978-1-909728-25-7

Printed in Great Britain

Instant Apostle is a new way of getting ideas flowing, between followers of Jesus, and between those who would like to know more about His Kingdom.

It's not just about books and it's not about a one-way information flow. It's about building a community where ideas are exchanged. Ideas will be expressed at an appropriate length. Some will take the form of books. But in many cases ideas can be expressed more briefly than in a book. Short books, or pamphlets, will be an important part of what we provide. As with pamphlets of old, these are likely to be opinionated, and produced quickly so that the community can discuss them.

Well-known authors are welcome, but we also welcome new writers. We are looking for prophetic voices, authentic and original ideas, produced at any length; quick and relevant, insightful and opinionated. And as the name implies, these will be released very quickly, either as Kindle books or printed texts or both.

Join the community. Get reading, get writing and get discussing!

Disclaimer

The data on which this book is based derives from a series of surveys carried out by and on behalf of the Evangelical Alliance. This data remains the intellectual property of the Evangelical Alliance. In line with our confidentiality agreement, the respondents remain anonymous and their answers and comments are unattributable. The secondary analyses, interpretations of the data and views of the authors of the individual chapters are theirs alone. Therefore opinions expressed in this work should not be taken as those of the Evangelical Alliance, its leadership team, Board or Council.

About the authors

Greg Smith – Editor
Greg is Research Manager with the Evangelical Alliance and is also a William Temple Foundation Associate Research Fellow. He has published extensively over many years on the subjects of sociology of urban religion and inner city mission and ministry.

Chapter authors

Rev Dr Steve R. Holmes
Steve is a Baptist minister and Senior Lecturer in Theology at the University of St Andrews. He chairs the Evangelical Alliance's Theology Advisory Group (TAG).

Dr Mandy Robbins
Mandy is a Reader in Psychology in the Department of Psychology, Glyndwr University, Wrexham.

Dr Matthew Guest
Matthew is Senior Lecturer in Theology and Religion at Durham University.

Dr Keith J. White
Keith is Visiting Tutor at Spurgeon's College, Malaysia Baptist Theological Seminary and Asian Graduate School of Theology.

Dr Sylvia Collins-Mayo
Sylvia is Head of the Department of Criminology and Sociology at Kingston University.

Professor William K. Kay
William is Professor of Theology at Glyndwr University, Wrexham.

Dr William Ackah
William is a lecturer in Community and Voluntary Sector Studies in the Department of Geography, Environment and Development Studies at Birkbeck College, University of London.

Dr Dave Landrum
Dave is the Director of Advocacy at the Evangelical Alliance.

Contents

Foreword

Steve Clifford, General Director, Evangelical Alliance

When we decided more than five years ago to begin the *21st Century Evangelicals* research, our aim was to produce a snapshot of the beliefs and practices of evangelical Christians in the UK. The first survey gathered data from more than 17,000 people, most of whom were evangelicals. The initial report, launched in 2011, painted a picture of a faithful and active constituency making a significant contribution to the life of the United Kingdom.

Since then our research team has carried out 16 quarterly online surveys, led by research manager Greg Smith and supported by ten Alliance member organisations. Many who took part in the initial survey joined our online research panel, which has now grown to close to 4,000 people, about half of whom regularly complete our questionnaires. We are grateful for the efforts of our partners and of all the respondents, without whom this work would be impossible.

A dozen thematic reports have been published which together give an amazingly positive and diverse picture of evangelicals in the UK today. The reports have been well received and have sparked conversations and ideas in churches across the UK, helping church leaders understand their congregations and make more effective plans for mission and ministry today. In the words of John Glass, General Superintendent of Elim Pentecostal Churches and Alliance Chair of Council:

> Once again, through precise analysis and helpful insight, the Evangelical Alliance has provided us with a reliable lens through which we can better understand the context in which we seek to serve – and so enabling us to focus with clarity on issues we should prioritise.

This book allows us to reflect more deeply on the significance of our findings through carefully compiled chapters written by a group of leading academics in sociology of religion and theology. These are academics who have generously supported the *21st Century Evangelicals* research programme over many years. They have drawn on their expert knowledge as scholars in their specialist fields, studied in depth the data we have gathered and written chapters in a style that is easily accessible. I would like to thank them for their hard work, and also to acknowledge the contributions of the church leaders and practitioners who have offered a brief response to each chapter.

I commend this book and hope you will enjoy reading it. It shows that evangelical Christianity in the UK remains vibrant and engaging, both counterculturally and incarnationally, in national, economic, social and local community life as well as connecting internationally within the global Christian family. While the book points out numerous issues that the church as a whole needs to address with some urgency, it is above all a testament of hope. It shows that our faith as evangelical Christians is not merely about what happens after we die, but is also a vibrant force for the transformation of lives and communities in the here and now.

Introduction: The *21st Century Evangelicals* Research Programme

The Evangelical Alliance is the largest and oldest body representing the UK's two million evangelical Christians. For more than 165 years we have been bringing Christians together and helping them listen to, and be heard by, the government, media and society.

In 2010 the Evangelical Alliance committed itself to a major research programme which would enable it to understand more fully the lives and concerns of its constituency of evangelical Christians across the United Kingdom. In order to shape and finance this work, we drew together a partnership involving selected member organisations of the Alliance who met regularly to plan and reflect on the research. The organisations who at various times have been members of this 'Research Club' include:

- Care
- Care for the Family
- Christians Against Poverty
- Compassion
- CWR
- MAF
- Open Doors
- Prospects
- Stewardship
- Urban Saints
- Wycliffe Bible Translators

In 2010, more than 17,000 people connected in some way with evangelical churches and networks completed a questionnaire about their beliefs, religious practices, opinions on political and moral questions, and their involvement and activism in the community. More than 12,500 of them defined themselves as evangelical Christians. Paper questionnaires were distributed at major Christian events and festivals and through a sample of EA member churches across the UK. A summary report of this research was published in January 2011.

Subsequently a research panel, recruited in the first place from the 17,000, has been asked to take part in online surveys four times each year. Each wave of the survey concentrated on a specific theme or topic known to be of interest to the Alliance and/or its member organisations and churches. More than 1,150 people responded to the first online survey, conducted around Easter 2011; in the *Life in the church?* survey carried out in February 2012, more than 1,864 replies were analysed.

January 2011 saw the launch of *21st Century Evangelicals* – a ground-breaking report in popular format. But this was just the beginning – a snapshot. Since then each survey has led to the publication of a report booklet, widely distributed in print and online, alongside accompanying materials such as PowerPoint presentations and discussion guides. The reports have been widely welcomed and have received many warm commendations from church leaders. All can be downloaded from the Evangelical Alliance website.[1]

An overview of our research reports so far:

- *Are we good neighbours?* survey conducted in February 2014; report published in August 2014.

- *Time for discipleship?* survey conducted in November 2013; report published in April 2014.

- *Working faithfully?* survey conducted in May 2013; report published in October 2013.

- *Life in the church?* survey conducted in February 2013; report published in May 2013.

- *Do we value education?* survey conducted November 2012; report published February 2013.

---

[1] http://www.eauk.org/ (accessed 12th December 2014).

- *Confidently sharing the gospel?* survey conducted August 2012; report published November 2012.

- *Does money matter?* survey conducted May 2012; report published September 2012.

- *The world on our doorstep?* survey conducted February 2012; report published May 2012.

- *Are we communicating?* survey conducted August 2011; report published December 2011.

- *How's the family?* survey conducted November 2011; report published February 2012.

- *Does belief touch society?* survey conducted Easter 2011; report published September 2011.

- *21st Century Evangelicals* survey conducted throughout 2010; report published January 2011.

In order to ensure the quality of our research we brought together an academic advisory group which included some of the leading social scientists who specialise in the study of religion in Britain and who have a particular interest in and connections with the evangelical church constituency. Most of the authors who have contributed to this volume have been members of the advisory group and have participated in the construction of questionnaires and the shaping of the published reports.

The aim of this book is twofold. Firstly, we want to draw together the findings from the different surveys to paint a panorama of evangelicalism in the UK in the early part of the twenty-first century. Secondly, we want to reflect more deeply than has been possible in the short popular survey reports, in the light of our understandings from the social sciences, on the significance of our findings for church and society, and on possible future scenarios for Christianity in this country.

We are aiming to write in an accessible style and to address the concerns of church leaders and ordinary Christians who are concerned to make their churches and their individual lives more effective in communicating the gospel and influencing and serving wider society. To help apply our findings and reflections in the everyday world, we have asked a number of well-known Christian practitioners to offer a short response to the issues raised in each chapter.

We hope this book will be a good read, and that it will be informative and provocative to your thinking and discipleship.

Preamble: Who are the evangelicals?
A demographic portrait

Greg Smith

The first question many people will want to ask is: How many evangelical Christians are there in the United Kingdom *today*? Estimates vary from the 5.5 million mentioned in Wikipedia to the ballpark figure of two million which is regularly used by the Evangelical Alliance. This figure is derived from a Tearfund survey in 2007 in which 7,000 people were interviewed. Among the regular churchgoers surveyed, a little more than a quarter (27%) self-identified as evangelical.

The reality is that no one (other than God) really knows, as there has never been a census or a reliable representative survey of the population in which people have been asked whether they are an evangelical Christian. Counting evangelicals would be a methodological nightmare. In the first place, definitions of the term can vary. While we might like to use a theological definition based on a statement of faith such as that of the Evangelical Alliance, the reality is that many people who are involved in evangelical churches, and who are happy to call themselves evangelicals, may not understand or believe everything expressed in such theological documents. Theologians themselves may have different understandings of what is essential for evangelical faith.

Neither is it possible to derive statistics about evangelicals from church attendance or membership figures. For evangelical believers are found in almost all the Christian denominations, in congregations which may or may not be easily described as evangelical in ethos and belief. And many of the newer independent and emerging churches, including those that mainly serve ethnic minority communities, are hard to track down and not particularly concerned with collecting or publicly reporting their statistics.

In any case, should we count only those people who are on membership lists, or those who are in church (once or twice) on a particular Sunday, or those who attend worship (at any time in the week) at least once in a month? Should we also count the children of families who belong to a church? How do you count people who might attend one church on a Sunday morning and another in the evening, or for a midweek service or Bible study?

However, some things are more easy to establish about the evangelical constituency in the UK. Perhaps the most significant is that in a context where all the indicators of the influence of Christianity are in decline, evangelicalism is relatively thriving. The proportion of the population who label themselves as Christian in the national Census declined from 72% in 2001 to 59% in 2011. In the mainline denominations, membership and attendance figures suggest a long-term decline in active participation in church life, and a rapid ageing of congregations. Within the main Protestant denominations, the majority of congregations that are surviving, thriving and even growing are those with an evangelical ethos. Most of the new congregations founded in recent decades, and most of the ministries that have proved to be effective among younger people, are charismatic or Pentecostal in style and evangelical in belief. In multicultural urban areas, the rapid growth of churches among diaspora communities in Britain reflects the vitality of Christianity in the global south, and much of it is evangelical in emphasis, though the Roman Catholic church, Orthodox churches and mainline Protestant denominations have also benefited.

All the data in our research programme is based on samples of volunteers who responded to our requests to complete questionnaires. The invitations were targeted through Evangelical Alliance networks and asked for committed Christians who were willing to take part. The baseline survey was carried out largely among people attending major evangelical festivals and gatherings such as Spring Harvest, New Wine, Keswick and Clan, and supplemented by batches of questionnaires completed by the congregations of a sample of Alliance member churches. There were more than 17,000 respondents in all, among whom a little more than 12,500 were self-defined evangelicals.

Subsequently, our aim was to build a panel of respondents who would respond regularly to online surveys. Invitations to take part were emailed to about 3,000 of the baseline survey respondents who had agreed to help and had provided valid email addresses. Over the following three years we continued to invite everyone from this list (other than those who requested to opt out, or whose email addresses became unusable) to take part in quarterly surveys. Additionally, we recruited new members through the Alliance's website, publications and email lists, and by a snowballing process whereby respondents were encouraged to forward details of our surveys to their contacts via email, social media and word of mouth in their church networks. By February 2014, personalised invitations were being sent to 3,934 email addresses. Around 1,500 questionnaires were completed for each survey (a response rate of more than 35%).

Our monitoring suggests that around 70% of people who completed one survey also completed the next one in the series, and that there was a group of several hundred regulars who completed all or most of the surveys.

Since our sample is based on self-selecting volunteers within a target population rather than on a random or carefully designed sample, we need to be very cautious in extrapolating from it to UK evangelicals as a whole. Additionally, because there is no reliable general data on the demographic make-up of the evangelical community in the UK, it is impossible to assess whether our samples are fully representative. However, it is possible to describe the demographic features of our panels and to make some judgements as to how these might fit with general, widely shared descriptions of the evangelical church.

In the following section we describe typical panels and suggest areas where we suspect there may be biases that make them a less-than-perfect match to the evangelical constituency in the church. Inevitably, because the panel's make-up changes from one survey to the next, we will only be able to speak about it in broad generalisations and with round numbers rather than with precise statistics.

Demographics

In the baseline survey, about 12,000 of the 17,000 people (71%) who took part in the research identified themselves as evangelical Christians. Reports from that survey concentrated on evangelicals, and in some cases made comparisons with the non-evangelical group. Typically in the panel surveys around 92% self-defined as evangelicals, with 5–6% not sure and 2–3% not evangelical (but committed Christians). This suggests that there is a penumbra of Christians who are linked with and well disposed to the broad evangelical movement, perhaps through their local church which has an evangelical ethos and leadership, but who may be uneasy about wearing the label.

Age

Our panels (especially the loyal members) are strongly weighted towards the middle-aged to young elderly age groups (i.e. those born before about 1960 make up 56% of our most recent survey respondents – February 2014). Again, this probably reflects the demographic of the UK church as a whole, and is probably particularly close to the age profile of Alliance members and networks.

Gender

Some of our panel surveys achieved a 50/50 gender balance, but in many cases it was around 55% male, and higher in the older age groups. This is a mismatch with the overall profile of the church, where women are in the majority. However, among panel members born after 1980, women outnumber men. This is probably linked to the pattern of use of digital technology, as older women are generally less likely than older men to be comfortable online.

Location

Most regions of the UK are adequately represented in our panel, though we seem to have consistently fewer members than we would expect in Northern Ireland, Wales and North East England. The sample appears to be weighted towards London (typically in our surveys 10%) and the South East of England (typically 20%), but so is the national population, and we suspect evangelical churches even more so.

Ethnicity

We have only occasionally asked about ethnicity (in February 2012 fewer than 5% said they had a heritage outside the UK, and in an internally reported Omnibus survey in May 2014 92% self-defined as white British). We think black and minority ethnic (BME) groups are represented in the sample at roughly the right level for the whole population of the UK, although probably under-represented in terms of the evangelical church which increasingly (especially in London and other metropolitan cities) is now majority BME. A very high proportion of BME Christians are evangelical or fundamentalist by theology, though they may not frequently use the 'evangelical' label, preferring to define themselves as Pentecostal.

Social class

We know that our panel is predominantly middle to upper class. (In our *Working faithfully?* survey in May 2013, 24% were higher professionals and a further 47% intermediate professionals.) We suspect this reflects the reality of the church in the UK as a whole. The church has always struggled to hold the loyalty of the working classes, and this is probably getting worse as inequality increases and secularising forces are at work. In our panel, the bias is likely to be increased because we operate online and with high expected levels of literacy.

A relatively high proportion of our panellists are public sector workers, especially among the women, where 27% work in education and 19% in health or social care. Around 24% of the men and 19% of the women work for the church or another Christian organisation.

Generally, the evangelicals in our panel are affluent. According to our *Does money matter?* survey carried out in May 2012, 25% have an annual household income of more than £50,000, and only 5% of less than £10,000 (who would most likely be older pensioners or students). There is a minority who are wealthy (20% with savings and investments not counting housing and pensions of more than £100,000) and a similar minority who are poor (18% with savings of less than £1,000).

Mostly, the Protestant work ethic survives, debt is avoided and thrift adopted. Most are not trapped into patterns of conspicuous consumption. 'Earn all you can, save all you can and give all you can' (Wesley) seems to be the watchword. Around 57% of respondents owe nothing on a mortgage or home loan, and 58% have no other debts. (It is worth noting that the age profile of the panel could favour a relatively high proportion of people who have paid off their mortgage.) Approximately 43% said they receive no state benefits at all, and of those who do, for the most part they only draw universal benefits.

Education

Our *Do we value education?* survey in November 2012 shows that our panel members are highly educated on the whole, and place a high value on education: 70% have a university degree and 41% have postgraduate qualifications.

Denominations

Our panel and evangelicals generally are attending or in membership of a wide range of (Protestant) denominations. Anglicans usually make up approximately 30% of the panel, Baptists around 18% and charismatic independents about 18%. The next largest groups are independent evangelicals (10%), Free Church denominations (10%), Pentecostals (5%) and Church of Scotland (4%). Our hunch is that Pentecostals are under-represented, but this is associated with the ethnicity and class demographic of Pentecostalism which means they are less likely to hear of or wish to do our online surveys.

According to our *Life in the church?* survey (February 2013), 69% attend churches which they believe to be 'definitely evangelical'. Only 8% think that denomination is a very important factor when choosing which church to attend.

Chapter 1: Evangelical theology and identity

Stephen R. Holmes

Defining evangelical identity

Faced with a set of survey data about what (UK) evangelicals believe, two opposite errors are invited. One is to dismiss the results as anything other than an indication, as if it were needed, that our catechesis needs to improve: those who call themselves 'evangelical' do not in fact believe what evangelicals should believe, and we need to teach them better to put that right. The contours of evangelical identity are, on this account, clear, and those who wish to claim the term need to be instructed in them; if only 50% believe that hell is a place of eternal conscious pain, the other 50% need to be put right!

The other error is to embrace the results uncritically as determinative for what evangelicals really think, regardless of the positions leaders and gatekeepers insist on. The contours of evangelical identity are here infinitely malleable, defined only by the shifting sands of current opinion. If only 37% of evangelicals agree that abortion can never be justified, then leaders ought to stop talking about 'the evangelical position on abortion'.

Both these positions are attractive because evangelical identity is presently contested in the UK (and indeed elsewhere). It is not hard to find assertions about what is necessary to evangelical identity in print, online or in the text of sermons or speeches. Such assertions generally highlight theological or ethical positions that the author/speaker feels to be under threat, in an attempt to defend the position, or to make his/her readers/hearers appreciate the seriousness of the threat. The writer/speaker insists that to surrender this position, or to embrace the alternative view, is to cease to be 'evangelical'.

I have no doubt that such assertions are genuinely believed by their various proponents and are sincerely offered. However, as evidence for what it means to be 'evangelical', I doubt their worth. In my judgement they are generally best read as attempts to gain traction in an ecclesial debate. (It is similarly not difficult to find attempts to claim that evangelical identity does not in fact, despite appearances, exclude a novel or radical position, which is no doubt equally sincere, but is generally similarly political in effect.)

In the face of these political concerns, and the contested identity they point to, survey data that appears to show that some/many evangelicals have surrendered a crucial position can appear threatening or liberating, and can lead to an attempt to shore up, or to break open, dominant narratives of evangelical identity. Equally, survey data that shows that evangelical opinion has remained surprisingly monolithic on a given issue might appear comforting or discouraging in its suggestion that the party line has held in the face of debates.

To take two examples from our survey, someone who argues that a creationist position is necessary to evangelical identity (presumably on the basis that it is the only appropriate reading of the Scriptures) would find little encouragement in our data, where only 26% of evangelicals agree with the proposition, 'Evolution and Christianity are incompatible.' (This compares to 32% of the general British population who agree that the statement, 'God created the world sometime in the last 10,000 years' is either 'definitely' or 'probably' true (Spencer & Alexander, 2009).) On the other hand, only 16% of evangelicals disagree that, 'Homosexual actions are always wrong,' suggesting that the resilience of evangelical opposition to progressive accounts of sexual morality, now normative in culture, remains remarkably strong.

All these various attempts to capture the definition of 'evangelical' fail because the word is a descriptor which is uncontrolled in use but is profoundly historically determined. The Vatican is able to determine what counts as authentically Catholic Christianity (if not what counts as authentically catholic Christianity); the General Synod of the Church of England, under Parliament, has power to determine what it is to be Anglican. There is no similar body, however, that can claim to define the meaning of 'evangelical'. While the term has deep history in the monastic tradition (referring to the 'evangelical counsels' of poverty, chastity and obedience), and means simply 'protestant' in German usage, it began to be used in its currently popular sense in the UK around the middle of the eighteenth century to refer in general to those who embraced, and energetically promulgated, a new, highly experiential, ethically rigorous, ecclesiologically diverse and doctrinally conservative form of protestant Christianity.

To claim to be 'evangelical' is, in common English protestant usage, to assert some sort of continuity with this tradition. No one may arbitrate such a claim authoritatively – indeed, it is noticeable that those bodies which may most plausibly claim to be generally representative of evangelicalism, whether nationally or internationally, generally visibly refuse to claim the right to define the term. Even in acting to turn down a membership application, or to expel a person or an organisation, there is generally no official speculation (private partisans on both sides of the debate are less reticent) on whether that person/organisation should be allowed to call themselves 'evangelical', or whether the adoption of a particular position places them outside of the 'evangelical' fold. Rather, there is a judgement that they do not fit the membership criteria of the organisation. That said, given the term's historical use, the broad plausibility of a claim to be evangelical may be tested historically.

Academic definitions of evangelical identity have, therefore, inevitably been descriptive and essentially historical. The only way we can meaningfully determine what it is to be 'evangelical' is to examine the range of people and organisations who have claimed the word as a self-denomination and uncover what they share in common. New survey data will add to, but not replace, that investigation. We should not assume that the result of this exploration will be theological and/or ethical: it may be that certain practices, political attitudes or sociological factors are far more strongly associated with owning the title 'evangelical' than any beliefs. (To offer a trite example, evangelical Anglican clergy have, from fairly early on in the movement, been identifiable by certain changing patterns of liturgical dress. Sometimes this has been a particular style of clerical collar; sometimes a refusal to don the more ornate vestments. In the contemporary Church of England, a male priest preaching or celebrating the Eucharist in an open-necked shirt (no clerical collar; no tie) is almost certain to be evangelical.)

We should not, however, draw too hard a contrast between politically charged and historical descriptive definitions of evangelical identity. The historical definitions are not by any means politically neutral. To take just one doctrinal example, the location of evangelical beginnings in the revivals of the 1730s make the Wesleys, Whitefield and Edwards defining figures for the movement, and so emphasise a form of evangelical 'ecumenism' that is unwilling to let differences over church order, or over predestination, become important. Evangelicals may indifferently be Anglican or Congregationalist, Calvinist or Arminian.

A counterproposal (less well accepted academically at present) sees a basic continuity running from the Anglo-American Puritan movement through the revivals to the self-conscious evangelical identity of the nineteenth century (Haykin and Stewart, 2008). If this is correct, then Arminian evangelicalism is a minor aberration, not an equal root (as is, to a lesser extent, Anglican/episcopalian evangelicalism). It would be foolish to claim that partisans in the historical debate are serenely unaware of such political implications (and it would be utterly unfair to suggest that their positions are driven by them, rather than by a commitment to reading the historical evidence in the best possible way). The way we construct the history is determinative for our understanding of the movement, and we need to be honest about that.

Further, we must be alive to the potential for different accounts of evangelical identity at different periods of history, or in different geographical (or cultural or ecclesial) contexts. At present, for example, to refuse to describe the Bible as 'inerrant' is, at very best, to place oneself on the edges of the evangelical movement in the USA; but the term is a late coinage, never used by Edwards or Finney, and is virtually unused in the UK. To say that it is a significant mark of evangelical identity to believe in and stress the inerrancy of Scripture makes sense when talking about twentieth- (and early twenty-first-) century American evangelicalism, but not in other contexts.

In countries in Europe that historically have a Roman Catholic state church, evangelical identity has often (and understandably) been significantly shaped by opposition to Catholicism, leading to accounts of what it is to be 'evangelical' that might seem somewhat unbalanced to evangelicals in the UK or the USA.

For a third example, indicated in our survey, it has become increasingly acceptable within British evangelicalism in recent decades to question the doctrine of eternal conscious torment. Such questioning would have been regarded as not just wrong, but positively dangerous, by earlier generations.

With these caveats in place, we may note three academically significant definitions of evangelicalism. The first is the famous 'Bebbington Quadrilateral', offered by David Bebbington as the result of his magisterial historical survey of British evangelicalism. For all the divergences, disagreements and differences, Bebbington argued, British evangelicalism had been consistently crucicentric, conversionist, activist and biblicist (Bebbington, 1989).

A second, and rather different, account comes from Mark Noll, whose exploration of transatlantic evangelicalism stressed sociological and political connections. To be an evangelical, according to Noll, was to be involved and implicated in a set of communities of conversation. Evangelicalism, in this account, was and is a sociological, not a theological, phenomenon (Noll, 1986).

Finally, Timothy Larsen offers a definition which combines attention to the distinctive shape of evangelical piety with the particular historical locatedness of the evangelical revival. He offers a fivefold list, which begins by asserting that an evangelical is 'an orthodox Protestant', moves on to historical location ('stands in the tradition of the global Christian networks arising from the eighteenth-century revivals') and spirituality ('has a preeminent place for the Bible in her or his Christian life'), before returning to hover on the boundaries of doctrine and spirituality ('stresses reconciliation with God through the atoning work of Jesus Christ on the cross ... stresses the work of the Holy Spirit in the life of an individual') (Larsen, 2007).

It is worth noticing that my various words of caution above are all operative in considering these definitions. Bebbington's definition is explicitly geographically limited; other writers have applied it as a generic definition of worldwide evangelicalism, but clearly in origin it is not claimed to be such, and if it works well as such that is a happy coincidence (and, no doubt, a reflection of the importance of the UK in evangelical history). Noll's definition offers no theological/ethical content but stresses sociology. Each of the three definitions is historical and descriptive, claiming no prescriptive power.

Questioning evangelical theology

With these various caveats in place about the nature of evangelical theology, it is time to sketch an account of evangelical theology. Theologies are distinguished not just by what is believed, but also by what is held to be central and what to be peripheral. The distinctiveness of evangelical theology is not so much in what is believed, as Larsen's definition above proposes. Evangelicals are essentially 'orthodox protestants', although so are many others – but in the weight given to various beliefs. Historically, somewhere near the core of evangelical theology, was a deliberate de-emphasis of ecclesiology and a stress on soteriology and on the work of the Spirit in the believer's life. An evangelical Anglican believed in episcopacy, to be sure, but did not make this a defining issue for Christian fellowship. In an Anglo-Catholic stress on baptismal regeneration, by contrast, they would see a soteriological error which was at least profoundly concerning (see Ryle, 1885 for a statement of this sort of position). Similarly, there is still a tradition of confessional Presbyterianism which would distance itself from evangelicalism, not because of any doctrinal difference, but because of a different estimation of the importance of Calvinist soteriology and presbyterian church order.

This creates a problem for the sort of work we are doing with our surveys. We are generally testing what people believe, not the strength of that belief or its importance in their broader theology. This problem is not in principle unsurmountable, of course; it is possible to imagine a questionnaire to test these various facets. The questionnaire would be rather complex, however, and so would increase the chance of respondents misunderstanding what was being asked, leading to poor results.

In recent academic work, a number of writers have explored the concept of 'ordinary theology'. This is the lived, operative, probably unarticulated theology of a group, generally a local congregation, which is contrasted (at least potentially) with the formal theology espoused in statements of faith and the like (Astley, 2002; Astley & Francis, 2013; Rogers, 2007). Our definitions of evangelical theology are all already moving towards 'ordinary theology', whether they are the historically derived accounts of identity of Bebbington, Noll or Larsen, or the attempt to narrate evangelicalism theologically on the basis of particular patterns of doctrinal emphasis which I have sketched, following Ryle.

Historians are attempting to define what people who called themselves 'evangelical' actually believed. The data is of course skewed to writers and leaders and is therefore not a true 'ordinary theology', and proposals for doctrinal definition are given a prominence which Astley and others would not give them, but the procedure is still fundamentally descriptive of observed patterns of belief. In describing the 'weight' given to different doctrines, we are necessarily moving in the realm of lived belief: an evangelical Anglican church is distinguished from a non-evangelical Anglican church not by different stated beliefs – both are, at least in theory, committed to the Articles and the Prayer book as definitive of their belief and practice – but by the lived emphases on certain of the various shared beliefs. Ryle expresses his accounts of these lived patterns with serene confidence and little evidence, but his claim to evangelical identity still relies on lived theology, not claimed statements of belief.

All of this suggests that, for the student of evangelical theology, the survey data is of great importance. A student of Roman Catholic theology has a body of official dogma to work with; data demonstrating that the beliefs of Catholics on the ground are not always in line with that dogma are no doubt interesting, but not finally decisive. Someone studying evangelical theology, however, has only the lived faith of evangelicals, now and in history, on which to reflect and build. Whatever the problems, this material is invaluable for any intellectually serious account of British (and Northern Irish) evangelical theology in the early twenty-first century.

The data

Preliminary comments

That said, there are genuine problems with discerning theology from surveys. Often, important technical theological distinctions are made by the choice of a specific phrase, or 'term of art'. If we were confident our respondents all had the level of theological education necessary to recognise these specific terms and the issues they denote, we could ask about them with confidence; lacking this confidence, we are faced with a potential problem.

This problem is visible in one of our surveys. Given the proposition, 'Abortion can never be justified,' our respondents were ambivalent, perhaps surprisingly so (37% agree; 18% unsure; 45% disagree). Although in the late 1960s UK evangelicals were largely indifferent to the 1967 Abortion Act, opposition to abortion became normal in the 1970s and rapidly became a defining mark of the movement, at least in its public presentation. Given this, this survey data might be read to suggest that the public leadership of the movement never carried the 'rank and file' with it in its opposition to abortion, or that there has been another cultural shift away from a pro-life commitment.

As someone who has taught undergraduate Christian ethics, I am very conscious that 'abortion is always wrong' will be heard in a very particular way by people who have studied the subject formally. Many textbooks illustrate at length a number of interesting limit cases around the subject of abortion. One example would be a (hypothetical) medical situation where doing nothing would inevitably result in the deaths of both mother and child, but performing an abortion would save the mother's life. There is an argument that, even in this case, the abortion should not be performed. (Essentially, if one understands abortion to be simply murder, murdering in cold blood is an evil act, even if a great good might result from it, and so it should not be done.) On this basis we routinely set examination questions for students, asking, 'Is abortion always wrong?' and we expect them to explore these hard limit cases.

Now, I have no idea whether problems like this were in the minds of any of our respondents, and if they were, of how many. It may be that UK evangelicals are far more accepting of abortion than of same-sex relationships or of assisted suicide. It may be that they are fairly hard-line on abortion in general but are prepared to make exceptions following rape, or in the case of certain severe disabilities, and so refuse the word 'always'. Further work – which could be questionnaire based, listing possible scenarios and asking about the licitness of abortion in each case – would be necessary to discover which of these explanations is right. I offer the comments above as an example of the danger that exposure to particular technical theological or ethical debates could lead to a skewing of our results in one direction or another.

The Bible

We have interesting data on the Bible: three questions that generated significantly different responses. Asked whether, 'The Bible, in its original manuscript [sic], is without error,' 53% of respondents strongly agree. Asked if, 'The Bible has the supreme authority in guiding my beliefs, views and behaviour,' 77% agree strongly. Asked if, 'The Bible is the inspired Word of God,' 87% agree strongly.

These questions expose a basic, and I believe significant, geographical division in evangelical theology. As noted above, 'inerrancy' – the doctrine that the Bible is without error – is a crucial belief, operating almost as a boundary marker for the constituency, for US evangelicalism. In the UK, the universal confession in significant evangelical statements of belief is rather the 'authority' of the Bible. (I have offered evidence for this division, and reasons for believing it to be more than merely verbal, in my Laing Lecture (Holmes, 2009).)

Now, I have also argued that a commitment to biblical authority probably requires a commitment to biblical inerrancy, logically speaking, and a commitment to inspiration underlies them both, but these are relatively subtle theological points which we should not expect people to grasp intuitively. Again, the question of the extent to which various ideas were consciously in people's minds as they answered the questions is not irrelevant: it is not hard to imagine someone aware of the importance of inerrancy in US evangelicalism and, wanting to be distanced from the American 'Religious right' picture of what it is to be evangelical, not responding to our question about error in the Bible on the basis of their own theological commitments but instead seeing it as a way of distancing themselves from a vision of evangelicalism they find profoundly distasteful. I have no evidence that even one person responded like that; it seems intuitively plausible to me that some might have done, however.

Conversionism and soteriology

Asked if, 'Jesus is the only way to God,' our respondents were remarkably vigorous in their affirmation: 91% of those who self-identified as evangelical strongly agree (and another 4% agree a little) in our baseline survey of 12,000. (In the follow-up survey on evangelism, 97% agreed with the same statement. This perhaps suggests that those who agreed to take part in follow-up surveys – or those who chose to respond to the one on evangelism – are slightly more conservative than evangelicals as a whole.) Again, of course, this statement is theologically ambiguous: the intellectually interesting accounts of the availability of salvation in non-Christian religions in recent decades have stressed the uniqueness of Christ, but have postulated that faithful and moral Hindus (say) may be saved through the work of Jesus without ever knowing His name or story (Rahner, 1969). We might surmise that this level of theological sophistication is beyond most of our respondents, but we cannot know that.

UK evangelicals are very committed to conversion still, with 94% insisting that rebirth is necessary to salvation and the same proportion agreeing that conversion leads to transformation of life. The classic evangelical themes of conversion and sanctification clearly remain strong.

Asked about the gospel, there is some interesting confusion: 89% agree that, 'The central message of the gospel is that on the cross Jesus bore the punishment for my sins,' but 73% agree that, 'The central message of the gospel is the kingdom of God' – both groups skewed towards older age ranges. It is a boring but nonetheless significant logical point that there can be only one 'central message'. A significant number – perhaps a majority – of our older respondents, however, are determined to have at least two 'central messages'.

Positively, we may read this as an affirmation that evangelicals, rightly or wrongly, remain viscerally committed to penal substitutionary accounts of the atonement, and are also deeply committed to visions of the coming kingdom being inaugurated through Jesus' death and resurrection. The logical problem of many respondents choosing two 'central messages' should not obscure this basic finding. The academic theologian might find in this data some encouragement for the contemporary fashion of interpreting the atonement in multiple ways (Gunton, 1988). Contemporary UK evangelicals, at least, instinctively reach for more than one metaphor to describe the work of Christ, and are happy to bend the rules of logic to insist on the importance of each of the various metaphors.

What are we saved from? There is visible nervousness about hell in our survey. As I have already noted, a bare 50% offer any agreement to the proposition that hell is a place of eternal conscious torment. At the same time, when offered the proposition, 'God's love is so wide and unconditional that He will welcome everyone into His Kingdom,' 43% agree. The statement is not straightforward, but at least invites the interpretation that it is an expression of universalism. It must, of course, be set against the very strong insistences that rebirth is necessary to salvation; again, our respondents are not compelled to fit in with our ideas of what is logically consistent. That said, a (we might say, properly evangelical) stress on the mercy of God is evident in our responses.

Given the straightforward question, 'Is the motivation for evangelism rescuing people from the danger of hell?' only 12% agree strongly, with another 23% agreeing; 27% are unsure; 28% disagree and 10% disagree strongly. Our respondents believe very strongly in the necessity of evangelism and conversion, but – rightly or wrongly – do not see hell as the primary motivation for that. They are also committed to affirmations of the broadness of divine mercy. If there is a logical problem here, it is not clear that it is being felt significantly strongly to make people change their views.

Tribalism

Evangelicalism is fissiparous, often giving rise to what Pete Ward has termed 'tribes' (1997). In one of our surveys we offered evangelicals a set of descriptors, the results of which were interesting. Unsurprisingly, relatively neutral descriptors that could be owned by any tribe were most popular ('Bible-believing Christian'; 'born-again Christian'). The next most popular choice was, 'I don't like labels – I'm just a Christian' (41% would describe themselves this way; another 26% would accept it as a description). Tribal identifiers were generally unpopular: 'Open evangelical' (12%) and 'Conservative evangelical' (11%) were the only two to get more than 10% of the sample saying they describe themselves using the terms (although in both cases another 20%+ would accept the term as a designation). 'Charismatic' was the exception, being owned or accepted by more than half the respondents (and rejected by 13%).

Unsurprisingly, perhaps, 'Fundamentalist' was an unpopular choice: only 3% would self-designate that way, and 37% would definitely reject the term. James Barr and Harriet Harris have claimed that UK evangelicalism is basically fundamentalist (Barr, 2010; Harris, 1998). More recent scholarship has rejected this, tracing carefully the sociological and theological differences in the movements while noticing small and isolated examples of patterns of faith that can reasonably be called fundamentalist within evangelical history (Bebbington & Jones, 2013). Our survey data suggests that this more recent scholarship matches the self-perception of evangelicals. Of course, even the basic term 'evangelical' has negative connotations, and I suspect many of our respondents would be happier saying they accept it as a designation rather than choose it as self-description.

One striking feature of the 'tribal' questions was the extent to which terms were unrecognised. When respondents were offered, 'I don't know what this means' as a response to the descriptors, 23% professed ignorance of 'Radical evangelical', 28% of 'Reformed evangelical', 29% of 'Open evangelical' and 36% of 'Post-evangelical'. The only 'tribal' term that was well understood was 'Conservative evangelical', but even there 10% stated they do not know what it means. The frequency and ease with which these terms are used on social media and in blog discussions might make us expect them to be more instantly recognisable, but it would seem that well-drawn online battle lines do not have as much immediate purchase among the generality of evangelicals as their partisans might suppose.

Conclusion

Our survey data suggests that UK evangelicals fit well within the standard definitions of evangelical identity still, and so suggests no need to revise those definitions. A focus on the inspiration and authority of the Bible – and a living out of that in reading and being guided by Scripture – is still a distinctive and normative aspect of evangelical theology, spirituality and identity. A belief in the saving power of the cross, and that conversion results in a transformed life, is equally, or even more, strong. These commitments are the heart of evangelical identity historically, and remain so in the UK today.

References

Astley, Jeff. *Ordinary Theology: Looking, listening and learning in theology* (Farnham: Ashgate, 2002)

Astley, Jeff & Francis, Leslie J. eds. *Exploring Ordinary Theology: Everyday Christian believing and the church* (Farnham: Ashgate, 2013)

Barr, James. *Fundamentalism* (London: SCM, 2010)

Bebbington, David W. *Evangelicalism in Modern Britain: A history from the 1730s to the 1980s* (London: Routledge, 1989)

Bebbington, David & Jones, David Ceri. eds. *Evangelicalism and Fundamentalism in the United Kingdom During the Twentieth Century* (Oxford University Press, 2013)

Gunton, Colin E. *The Actuality of Atonement: A study in metaphor, rationality, and the Christian tradition* (Edinburgh: T & T Clark, 1988)

Harris, Harriet A. *Fundamentalism and Evangelicals* (Oxford University Press, 1998)

Haykin, Michael A. G. & Stewart, Kenneth J. eds. *The Emergence of Evangelicalism: Exploring historical continuities* (Nottingham: IVP/Apollos, 2008)

Holmes, Stephen R. 'Evangelical Doctrines of Scripture in Transatlantic Perspective: the 2008 Laing Lecture' *Evangelical Quarterly* (2009)

Larsen, Timothy. 'Defining and locating evangelicalism' in Timothy Larsen and Daniel J. Trier (eds.), *The Cambridge Companion to Evangelical Theology* (Cambridge University Press, 2007)

Noll, Mark. *Between Faith and Criticism: Evangelicals, Scholarship, and the Bible in America* (San Francisco: Harper and Row, 1986)

Rahner, Karl. 'Anonymous Christians' in *Theological Investigations* VI (tr. K. H. Kruger and B. Kruger) (London: Darton Longman and Todd, 1969), pp.390–398

Rogers, Andrew. 'Reading Scripture in Congregations: Towards an Ordinary Hermeneutics' in Walker, Andrew and Bretherton, Luke. eds. *Remembering our Future: Explorations in Deep Church* (Milton Keynes: Paternoster, 2007), pp.81–107

Ryle, J. C. *Knots Untied* (1885).

Spencer, Nick & Alexander, Denis. *Rescuing Darwin: God and evolution in Britain today* (Theos, 2009)

Ward, Pete. 'The Tribes of Evangelicalism' in G. Cray, et al. *The Post-Evangelical Debate* (London: SPCK/Triangle, 1997), pp.19–34

Response to Stephen Holmes' 'Evangelical theology and identity'

Lucy Peppiatt

Stephen Holmes' analysis of the responses to a survey on 'evangelical theology and identity' make for interesting reading. I was not sure what to expect among the data collected, and I have to admit to having wondered even about the endeavour, so it was even more interesting to see what emerged. The results strike me as a mixture of the predictable and the surprising. Perhaps that in itself should not be surprising!

It is extremely helpful to have Stephen's interpretative lenses on the data, providing a brief historical sweep of the landscape and making what I believe to be fair assumptions in relation to how questions 'might' have been interpreted by the participants. Despite his spelling out of the very clear limitations on defining the term 'evangelical', there clearly are identifiable threads of continuity among the characteristics of evangelicals, and this is evident in their 'ordinary theology', or the realm of 'lived belief'. I was particularly struck by the insightful comment that theologies 'are distinguished not just by what is believed, but also by what is held to be central and what to be peripheral'. How true. Not only this, but it is always instructive also to take the time to notice what is not being said, or perhaps what is never being said in any given community. Beliefs and identity can also be constructed by the gaps.

The predictable elements, then, were perhaps to hear that evangelicals focus on the inspiration and authority of the Bible, and on the saving power of the cross to transform the lives of those who turn to a living faith in Jesus Christ. The surprise was perhaps that which was left on the periphery, including the resistance to or even ignorance of 'tribal' definitions. Overall, I found these heartening findings. First, it is a good thing that there are Christians who self-identify as those who claim that the Bible is 'authoritative' and who see the saving and transforming power of Jesus Christ crucified and resurrected as the good news of the Christian faith. Second, this surely must be a strong basis for unity where it is so easy to focus on the things that divide, the latter point being bolstered by the reality that self-confessing evangelicals on the whole are resisting the divisive labels. This, too, is very good news!

My final reflection as a pastor of many years now, and as a theological educator for a few years, is that despite claims about the centrality and authority of Scripture, the amount of engagement with the Bible for normal evangelical Christians is, in fact, minimal. I have no idea whether this discrepancy is also a thread of continuity through the years or whether it is a new thing, but with so many resources now available, it strikes me as a gap worth closing between our confessed beliefs and our practices.

Lucy Peppiatt is the Principal of Westminster Theological Centre.

Chapter 2: Life in the church
Mandy Robbins and Greg Smith

There was, until recently, a widely held view that religion in the UK is in inexorable decline, as church attendance fell, church membership showed signs of ageing, proportions of the population professing belief in God were in retreat and the influence of Christian churches diminished. This was the 'secularisation thesis,' which some scholars of religion such as Steve Bruce (2002) presented in a hard form. According to this view, the long-term future of Christianity was bleak indeed.

Headline statistics still suggest the decline continues – for example, the 2011 Census records 59% of the population who identified as Christian compared with the 2001 figure of 72%. Recorded weekly attendance in the major denominations continued to fall – for example, the Church of England recorded an average of 1.03 million adult attenders in 2000 but only 898,000 in 2010. In Methodism over three years, from 2007 to 2010, the number of open churches fell by 4%, membership by 10%, the community roll by 12%, baptisms and thanksgivings by 7%, marriages and blessings by 12%, average adult Sunday attendance by 7%, and average adult midweek attendance by 11%. Peter Brierley's (2012) monitoring of denominational membership trends over four decades confirms a general pattern of decline in the major denominations, with a few more encouraging figures among Pentecostals, Orthodox, new (usually charismatic) churches, and 'fresh expressions' congregations.

This picture may not, however, tell us the complete story of Christian faith in Britain today. The Church of England takes comfort that 1.7 million people take part in Church of England services each month, a level that has been maintained since the turn of the millennium, and that across England each year three people in ten attend regular Sunday worship at least once. Attendance at Cathedral services has been rising for several years, and in London there has been considerable church growth across many denominations, although much of this is linked to the super-diversity of the capital as a global city and the gathering into congregations of people who already had a strong Christian faith (see, for example, the work of David Lankshear, *Signs of Growth*). David Goodhew (2012) has brought together a number of accounts and reflections on stories of church growth across the UK, which suggest that the tide of secularisation may not be sweeping everything before it.

Because of this and other factors, most sociologists of religion today present a softer and more nuanced version of the secularisation thesis. Rather than seeing decline as a one-way street, they explore a transformation of the religious landscape, and some even think of our contemporary social environment not as post-Christendom so much as post-secularity. Linda Woodhead and Rebecca Catto (2012) present a series of essays which explore the changes currently afoot. The general trend seems to be away from participation in institutionalised and formal religion in which establishment Christianity was the dominant force, towards a more diverse society in which religious identity and belonging remain significant for many, but where patterns of believing are more personalised. These may sometimes draw on Christian sources and mix with beliefs and practices from Western secular and other faith-based cultures.

Many evangelicals would want to critique this approach to faith as individualised consumer religion rather than loyalty to the revealed truth of Scripture. Yet at the same time, evangelical Christianity has always had an ability to translate and present the gospel in culturally diverse forms, in becoming in the words of Paul 'all things to all people so that by all possible means I might save some' (1 Corinthians 9:19-23). In many cases this has led to significant church growth, yet it has sometimes attracted the criticism that it is niche marketing rather than fulfilling Christ's commission to make disciples of all nations.

Many, though not all, of the success stories of thriving churches in Britain today are found within evangelicalism. Evangelicals, it seems, remain more hopeful about the future of the church and more committed to the corporate expression of the Christian faith, through regular church attendance, active participation in worship and learning together, financial support of the church, and engagement in mission and service. Anglicans often refer to the five marks of mission, which they hope to find in every local church, as:

- To proclaim the Good News of the Kingdom

- To teach, baptise and nurture new believers

- To respond to human need by loving service

- To seek to transform unjust structures of society, to challenge violence of every kind and to pursue peace and reconciliation

- To strive to safeguard the integrity of creation and sustain and renew the life of the earth (Anglican Communion).

A commitment to mission in the wider world (especially in terms of the first four of these marks) is an important and probably defining feature of evangelical churches. However, in this chapter we will seek to explore, in the light of our survey findings, what life in the church means for evangelical church attenders today, and how they experience and participate in coming together as God's people.

The insights from the participants detailed in this chapter represent a total of 987 people who responded to the *Life in the church?* survey. It is based on a fresh analysis of the data so the statistics in this chapter will not always exactly match those that appeared in the published report (Evangelical Alliance, 2013). This sample is selected from a total of 1,682 participants. Because of the purpose of this analysis we did not include the 557 church leaders (although they do have a separate section within the chapter), the 55 who were married to a church leader or the 83 who did not complete the question that enabled us to ascribe them to the appropriate group.

Evangelicals in congregations

The remaining 987 participants represent eight denominational groups. Nearly a third (32%) attend Anglican churches, with a fifth attending Baptist and independent charismatic churches (19% each). More than one in ten (12%) attend 'other evangelical' churches, 7% attend free churches and 5% attend Pentecostal and Presbyterian churches. Only 1% report that they are not committed to any particular denomination at present. For most participants, their church is close by, with 33% reporting that their church is less than a mile from their home, 41% reporting that their church is between one and three miles from home, and 19% that their church is between four and ten miles from their home. The remaining participants travel to churches that are more than 11 miles away.

The evangelicals in this sample not only tend to attend a local church but also tend to be loyal to that church, with 31% having attended their church for more than 20 years. Only 7% have joined their church in the last year. When asked about the congregation they attend, the predominant characteristic is that they tend to be middle class, with 62% agreeing that this is the case. However, the presence of children is marked in these congregations, with 65% agreeing that there are lots of children and nearly half (46%) agreeing that they have lots of committed young people (under the age of 25). Nearly half (46%) report that their congregation is growing numerically. Sixteen per cent go to large churches with regular congregations of 300+, and 11% to small churches with fewer than 50 people attending.

Of the participants, 53% are female and 47% are male. This represents a very different profile to that seen in the Anglican churches, for example, where approximately two-thirds are female. Research in both the UK and the USA speaks of a 'feminisation' of our churches. This is clearly not the case for the evangelicals in our survey.

The age profile, however, is more in line with other Christian groups in the UK, with more than a quarter (26%) born before 1950, making them aged 63 or over, and a further quarter (26%) born in the 1950s. Moreover, 21% were born in the 1960s, 14% in the 1970s, 10% in the 1980s and 4% in the 1990s. Although evangelicals include greater numbers of younger members than other denominations, this difference is not as obvious as it is for gender. When considering the age profile it is necessary to keep in mind that this data was collected online as an opportunity sample, and this may have under-represented older people, particularly older women.

The following sections focus on four aspects of church life for evangelicals: their involvement in church life, their preferred style of worship, what aspects of church life they view as important, and their attitude towards their church leaders. In each section, an overview of results is presented, followed by an exploration of the data by gender and age. Exploring the data by gender enables consideration of notable differences between the experiences of church life among men and women. Exploring the data by age enables a focus on experience of church life by three different cohorts (those born before 1960, those born in the 1960s and 1970s, and those born since 1979) to ask whether age impacts people's experience of and engagement with church.

Involvement in church life

Overview

Evangelicals are frequent church attenders, with 79% attending a Sunday morning worship service at least once a week and a further 12% at least once a fortnight. Many are more than passive churchgoers – a quarter of the participants are involved in welcoming people on arrival (25%), a third are involved in leading worship (32%) and a fifth (20%) in providing music for worship. Many do more than one of these tasks. Outside of the services, involvement remains significant, with nearly half (47%) being involved in prayer groups, more than a quarter (27%) working with young people, and more than a quarter involved in social action projects (28%).

On the other hand, Sunday attendance does not necessarily translate into active involvement, especially perhaps for people with a busy lifestyle and work responsibilities, living in a mobile and individualised culture. As one respondent put it, 'Too many seem to want to turn up and have a good service on Sunday without becoming really involved with each other.' Another acknowledged that there is a 'need to motivate everyone to play their part' within the life of the church.

Gender differences

Evangelical men and women engaged in church life undertake roles traditionally associated with their gender. Men are significantly more likely to be involved in 'up front' leadership roles than women – for example, preaching at Sunday services (22% compared with 7%). Leadership within smaller groups is also significantly more likely to be undertaken by men – for example, leading a home group (34% compared with 26%). Women are more likely to lead in traditional female roles such as working with children and young people (34% compared with 18%) and providing refreshments (29% compared with 19%).

Age differences

Involvement in church life does present some interesting differences between the three age groups. The profile of older church members is one of personal support of other church members through pastoral visiting (22% compared with 7% in the middle age group and 5% in the youngest age group) and welcoming people on arrival (35% compared with 21% and 25% respectively). They are twice as likely as the youngest age group to be involved in cleaning or maintaining church buildings and grounds. Older church members are more outward looking than younger members, being twice as likely to be involved in working on overseas mission or international links.

Evangelistic outreach is more likely to be engaged in by the youngest age group (35%). Nearly half (49%) of the youngest age group are involved in working with young people, compared with 14% of the oldest age group.

This raises issues about intergenerational understanding between the different groups within churches, particularly given that certain areas of involvement seem to be dominated by different age cohorts. The middle age group are not as involved – perhaps because this is when people are busy raising their own family and working and so have less time to give to the church.

Another important issue is how far churches may be segregated by age. While it is hard to extract precise data about this from our surveys, general involvement in the evangelical church scene suggests there are some churches (especially in London and other university towns) which predominantly attract the 18–30 age group (students and young singles), many suburban and small town churches which focus on families with young children, and others in rural or retirement areas or in Urban Priority Areas outside London where congregations are composed mainly of over-50s.

Preferred styles of worship

Given that most of our participants are regular and frequent churchgoers, we need to explore what sort of worship evangelicals attend and enjoy. Nearly three-quarters report enjoying contemporary worship (73%) and communion services (71%). These are the two most important forms of worship to evangelicals. Contemporary worship (usually understood to include lots of relatively modern worship songs led by a worship group featuring guitars and an informal style) is very much associated with evangelicals, although communion services are less so.

Many people may assume that evangelicals will embrace new church initiatives, but the data from this survey does not support this as only 13% state that they take part in and enjoy 'fresh expressions' of worship such as messy church and café church – the two lowest-scoring styles of worship out of a possible 12 from which respondents were asked to select. However, for many evangelicals in our sample, these expressions of worship are simply not available to them, whereas contemporary worship and communion are available to nearly all. Perhaps it needs to be noted here that such activities tend to be seen as missional and targeted towards outsiders rather than towards churchgoing believers. As one participant identified, there can be a 'problem with mixed expectations of congregations in terms of worship and witness'. It might also be because evangelicals in our sample feel as this respondent expressed: 'Programmes, methods and the trendy thing has taken hold and there is no confidence in the power of God's gospel.'

Gender differences

Of the 12 styles of worship explored by the survey, only three areas present significant gender differences. Two of the three concern participation. More women than men note a preference for interactive/participatory worship (41% compared with 31%) and for charismatic/Pentecostal worship (36% compared with 30%). Given the findings above, that men are significantly more likely to be leading services from the front, it would seem that this is not because women do not wish to be involved. It could be that women are more inclined towards worship that can potentially involve the whole congregation rather than worship led from 'the front'. The third worship style that is more likely to appeal to women than men is healing services (27% compared with 19%), which may reflect a gender difference in respect of personal engagement with bodily health and well-being.

Age differences

Age makes no significant impact on any of the preferred worship styles. Thus, 70% of the oldest age group, 71% of the middle age group and 70% of the youngest age group state that they enjoy the communion service. With regard to contemporary worship, the percentages present a similar profile, with 70% of the oldest age group, 73% of the middle age group and 77% of the youngest age group agreeing that they enjoy this type of worship. Messy church and café church do not attract a larger percentage of younger participants than older participants, although literature on these newer forms of worship would suggest that this would be the case. There is no evidence, then, for generational differences in which styles of worship are enjoyed more than others.

Important aspects of church life

The participants were asked to consider what aspects of church life they consider to be important. For more than two-thirds, the most important thing is the theological and doctrinal stance of the church. There is also a recognition that such issues could cause division: one participant stated their hope as, 'We will remain open to some differences of opinion which do not affect the key doctrines of the faith without causing division.' There is a gap of 10% between the importance rating of this aspect of church and the next most important consideration for the respondents, which is the depth and relevance of Bible teaching to their personal growth (57%). Other aspects of church life cluster around this particular issue, including offering an inclusive welcome to everyone (56%), the quality of the relationship between members (56%), the standard of preaching (55%) and regular home groups for fellowship learning and prayer (50%). The importance placed on these aspects of church life is neatly summarised by one of the participants: 'Churches that preach the Bible clearly and consistently, love each other, pray much and work to serve those around them are the ones that grow.'

What is of very little importance is the type of building in which the church meets (2%), the quality of refreshments offered (2%) and the denomination to which the church belongs (5%). The emphasis is clearly on the teaching and a personal commitment to growing together in faith.

Gender differences

In line with the gender differences found with regard to preferred style of worship, women present a greater emphasis on the inclusivity of their church. For example, women are significantly more likely than men to report that an inclusive welcome to everyone is important (60% compared with 52%) and that the church is a place where a lot is happening (25% compared with 17%).

Inspirational leadership is more important to women (34% compared with 24%). Is this because they are unlikely to be doing the leading themselves? The women are consistent in that above we noted their involvement in working with young people, and here they are more likely to see it as more important than men see it (45% compared with 36%). Women also place greater emphasis on their own faith journey, with more importance being placed on regular home groups for fellowship, learning and prayer (55% compared with 43%), and the depth and relevance of Bible teaching to their personal growth (60% compared with 55%).

Age differences

Two significant findings emerge from the data when exploring the importance that the three different age groups place on what is important to them at church. Although the older age group are not as involved in working with young people, they are committed to seeing a programme of activities for children and young people provided by their church: nearly half (42%) agree that this is of value.

The other difference between the age groups is a concern with the theological and doctrinal stance of the church, where the youngest group see this as significantly less important (16%) than the other two age groups (32% for both).

Attitude towards church leaders

The majority of evangelicals have a positive view of their church leader, with 84% agreeing that they respect the authority of their leader, 64% saying they are inspired by their church leader and 75% agreeing that they strive to follow the advice of their church leader.

Much is written about the stress that church leaders are under, with the lack of balance between their public and private lives and the unrealistic expectations that congregations place on them. This was summarised by one participant who stated, 'The leadership aren't being looked after properly, thus those in the church suffer.' More than half of our respondents who are not themselves leaders (56%) agree that their church leader works too many hours, even though they perceive that the leader is actively drawing others in to build a broad team of people to take responsibility for leadership (77%). A third agree (31%) that their church leader should take more time off to relax.

Two findings would seem to be of concern: one in ten feels that their church leader seeks to control and dominate members of the congregation (12%). One respondent states, 'All too often, bullying by leaders goes unrecognised and unchallenged.' Conversely, one in ten feels that fellow members of the congregation have a somewhat unrealistic perspective of their church leader, expecting them to do everything and be a perfect saint (10%).

Gender differences

Evangelical men seem to have a different view of their church leaders than evangelical women. Men are significantly more likely to think that their church leader works long hours (61% compared with 52%). This may be because church leaders are more likely to be male and consequently men in the congregation have a greater identification with and understanding of the work involved in taking on leadership roles. Men are also significantly more likely to report that they consider their church leader to be a good personal friend (39% compared with 29%). Again, this would give them greater insight into the work involved in leadership.

However, this support from the men does not mean they are more likely to feel that their church leader is doing a good job. Indeed, the women are significantly more likely to agree that they are inspired by the example of their church leader (67% compared with 61%), and that they feel their church leader is excellent at preaching and teaching the Bible (74% compared with 68%). Maybe some men who are not church leaders feel they could do a better job themselves.

Age differences

Two significant differences emerge when the data is explored by age. Those in the youngest age group are significantly more likely to report that they are inspired by their church leader (74%) than either the middle age group (65%) or the older age group (58%). However, the older age group are more likely to pray for their leader (74%) compared with the middle age group (58%) and the youngest age group (45%). Perhaps those in the older age group feel a greater need to pray for their leader because they do not feel inspired by them. In spite of this, the older age group are more likely to feel that their church leader is excellent at pastoral ministry with members of the congregation (50%) and are more likely to count them as a good personal friend (39%).

Views from church leaders

For this section we have gone back to the same survey and explored the perceptions of the 557 church leaders with regard to some of the issues of leadership. More than half of evangelical churchgoers agree that their church leader works too many hours. Many church leaders in our survey work in teams, and a significant number do their church work (often unpaid) in addition to paid employment. Yet 23% of those in a team of leaders work between 11 and 20 hours for the church, 12% between 21 and 40 hours and 11% more than 40 hours.

However, if the hours worked are explored by those in sole leadership positions and those working in teams, the difference is stark. Nearly half (47%) of sole leaders work more than 50 hours a week compared with 7% of those who work in teams. Nearly a quarter (24%) agree that their relationships with their family and friends suffer because of the demands of ministry, and more than a third (38%) find it difficult to find time to relax. Despite this, the ministers have a positive perspective of the support they receive from their church communities, with 78% feeling supported and 76% willing to delegate tasks to a ministry team. Yet, while more church leaders feel supported and are willing to delegate, one in ten feels that the congregation expects them to do everything and to be a perfect saint.

For the leaders of congregations, the balance seems to be positive in that overall the majority of leaders (85%) agree that they greatly enjoy their ministry. The perspective of the leaders and those whom they serve seems to demonstrate a level of understanding of the impact the leadership role can have on both the leader and their personal life.

Conclusion

Broadly speaking, our survey suggests that evangelical Christians are strongly and loyally committed to their church, and that they devote much time, prayer and effort to participating in church life. They are also overwhelmingly upbeat and hopeful about the future and about the growth of their own fellowship, if perhaps more realistic about the prospects of the church in the UK as a whole. While it is obvious that those who have become disillusioned with or have left the church are unlikely to have taken part in our surveys, there is plenty of evidence that church involvement is a central and positive feature of the everyday life of most evangelicals.

It is clear that most are relatively unconcerned about the church as a building, or as an institution, and that for most evangelicals the importance of denomination is secondary. Much more important is the expectation that the core beliefs are in line with faithful interpretation and teaching of the Bible, and the sense of belonging to a caring and supportive Christian community where all kinds of people are welcomed and included.

However, some of our data seems to indicate that loyalty to perceived theological truth can be in tension with the aspiration to be an open and inclusive community which is forgiving and non-judgemental. There appear to be enough significant differences related to gender and age to suggest that older people and men are more likely to value theological truths, while women and younger people are more likely to value personal relationships and the sense of being an inclusive community. They are more likely to have an image of the church, as one respondent puts it, as 'inclusivity, diversity, acceptance … connectedness'. At one end of the spectrum, faith is about believing; at the other, it is more about belonging. This would entail a church which is about 'using people's gifts and feeling a part of something'. And here we are speaking about ordinary Christians 'in the pews' rather than about church leaders, who are more likely to be older men, and perhaps more concerned about beliefs and institutions.

Sometimes in the context of our contemporary consumerist, individualist society, evangelical churches are critiqued as being mere marketing machines, offering a religious product at a bargain price. One respondent put it like this:

> My own fear is that as numbers dwindle, the leadership will change the emphasis from a church that emphasises personal responsibility and personal mission to a church of entertainment and excitement.

However, while there is evidence that some people in our survey do have preferences in terms of worship style and the ethos of the church they would wish to attend, there is much to suggest that evangelicals are not simply consumers of a religious product. Rather they are believers who are concerned to attend a church where their religious understandings are reinforced by good Bible teaching, and disciples who wish to learn how to be better followers of Jesus. They are also, for the most part, concerned to be loyal members of a local faith community, and as members of that church to be involved in witness and service to the wider community. In fact, far from being individual consumers basing their participation in church primarily on the satisfaction of their own felt needs, they are likely to become co-producers of religious activities and products. To be actively involved is a core feature of the ethos of most evangelical churches in the UK.

Finally, we need to make a comment about the demographics of the typical evangelical church, or more precisely those who are accessible through the networks of the Evangelical Alliance. Our respondents generally recognise that their churches are predominantly middle class in make-up and culture. This may provoke a vague and slightly guilty concern, or sometimes a denial that class matters, especially as evangelicals hold very strongly that the gospel has a universal appeal, regardless of wealth, status, gender or ethnicity. History has shown that the British working class has not widely joined and become established in evangelical churches, or where they have they have moved up in society and moved out of working class neighbourhoods. This also means that most thriving evangelical churches, and the centre of gravity of evangelicalism as a movement, are located in the suburbs and smaller towns of South East England. There are some exceptions, with evangelicals showing a strong presence in Northern Ireland and in cosmopolitan inner London, and significant recent changes towards a church with global connections and ethnic diversity. Yet, evangelicalism in Britain, and its leadership in particular, still remains predominantly white, middle or upper class, male, well educated and affluent.

There is much talk of serving, influencing and transforming whole communities, yet as our other surveys on evangelism and discipleship have shown, most evangelicals lack opportunity, zeal and confidence to share their faith with unbelievers. The challenge for the church to achieve substantial conversion growth across the country, in the face of indifference, and to make an impact on society, remains immense.

References

Evangelical Alliance (2013). *21st Century Evangelicals: A snapshot of the beliefs and habits of evangelical Christians in the UK.* London: Evangelical Alliance.

Brierley, P. (2012). Church Statistics 2005–2015 – Introduction. Available at http://brierleyconsultancy.com/images/csintro.pdf (accessed 6th August 2014).

Bruce, S. (2002). *God is dead: Secularization in the west.* Wiley-Blackwell: London.

Goodhew, D. (2012) (ed.). *Church growth in Britain: 1980 to the present.* Ashgate: Farnham.

Lankshear, D. W. & Francis L. J. (2009). *Signs of Growth: Preliminary Report for the Woolwich Episcopal Area* London: Diocese of Southwark.

Lankshear, D. W. & Francis L. J. (2011). *Signs of Growth: Preliminary Report for the Kingston Episcopal Area* London: Diocese of Southwark.

Lankshear, D. W. & Francis L. J. (2012). *Signs of Growth: Preliminary Report for the Croydon Episcopal Area* London: Diocese of Southwark.

Woodhead, L. & Catto, R. (2012) (eds.). *Religion and change in modern Britain.* Routledge: London.

The Anglican Communion. Available at http://www.anglicancommunion.org/ministry/mission/fivemarks.cfm (accessed 24th December 2014).

Yes, there is life in the church: A response to chapter 2

John Glass

At the dawn of the twenty-first century, *The Economist* published God's obituary. Ten years later, John Micklethwait, its editor, and Adrian Wooldridge, its Washington bureau chief, produced *God is Back* – a portrait of the current global impact of both Christianity and Islam around the world. Given that one describes himself as a Catholic and the other an atheist, the book is not written from an evangelical perspective, but it is no less powerful for all that.

As I write, both *The Spectator* and the *Financial Times* have a feature on the growth of Christianity in China and point out that, while the church is experiencing accelerated persecution, there are now more practising Christians in China than registered members of the Communist Party (100 million to 86.7 million). Tim Phillips of *The Telegraph* has said that, at the current rate of growth, by 2030 there will be 250 million Christians in China, far outstripping the USA.

In this country, most commentators speak of 'demise' rather than 'rise' when referencing the church. However, as Greg and Mandy point out, the demographic is not consistent across all denominations. Though membership in some is in freefall, in others there is evidence of exponential growth and church planting. It would appear that what is good is getting better and what is not is getting worse – and it all comes down to focus.

When I was a theological strident in the late 1960s, among the books that had an impact on me was Michael Griffith's *Cinderella with Amnesia* which saw the church as the Bride of Christ. However, she had forgotten not only what and where the ball was but, more tragically, could not remember her own identity.

My close friend Dr Michael Ntumy, who at that time was the chairman of the largest Christian denomination in Ghana that now numbers more than two million, provided a perceptive insight as to why the church in Africa is growing while the church in the West is not. Among a number of reasons he proffered was the observation that when people join a church in Europe they join a congregation that takes the form of an audience, but when they become part of the church of Pentecost in Ghana, they join an army that has a focus.

The church in the UK has a choice: it either continues to take a consumerist route that centres around its members having their 'needs met', or it transitions its vision and values to face outwards. Unless its lens hones in on purpose and direction, we will witness the embalming of an organisation rather than the embracing of a living organism that was created to be the agent of societal change.

This is nowhere better illustrated than in the account on the Mount of Transfiguration when Moses and Elijah appear and talked with Jesus. Peter's initial reaction was to build three shelters to enshrine the mystical experience. Happily for the troubled young man at the foot of the mountain, Peter decided not to do so, as the salt is not for the saltshaker, the light for the bushel nor the ship for the harbour. His focus moved from blessing to purpose.

Perhaps the best definition for spirituality in the context of a church that desires to produce lasting fruit is its ability to take light from where it is to where it isn't – as subversive as salt and as penetrating as revelation.

John Glass is the General Superintendent of the Elim Pentecostal Church and chairman for the Council of the Evangelical Alliance.

References

Griffiths, M., *Cinderella with Amnesia*. Inter-Varsity Press, 1975.

Micklethwait, J. & Wooldridge, A., *God is Back: How the Global Rise of Faith Is Changing the World*, Allen Lane, 2009.

Chapter 3: Evangelicals and social involvement

Greg Smith

Evangelical Christians, since the movement bearing the name emerged in the eighteenth century, have been noted for their activism in preaching and spreading the gospel to the ends of the earth, and also in their work for social reform and charitable care. In the nineteenth century, great public figures such as William Wilberforce and Lord Shaftesbury led the struggle to abolish slavery and child labour and, along with others such as Barnardo, Muller and William and Catherine Booth, were involved in founding charitable organisations covering every conceivable form of human need.

In the twentieth century, commitment to social involvement was more patchy as some feared that the social gospel could divert people away from the foundational truths about eternal salvation. Yet by the end of the century, a more holistic approach was re-emerging with the establishment of organisations such as Tearfund and the wide acceptance across the evangelical world of the Lausanne Covenant of 1974. This was drafted by a group which included the highly influential John Stott, who died in 2013 and who was the most frequently named speaker and author (by 15% of respondents) in our *Time for discipleship?* survey. Our research suggests that this tradition of active, socially engaged evangelicalism is alive and well, and continuing to make a significant impact on the life and welfare of British society in the twenty-first century.

Under the New Labour government (1997–2010), the theoretical concept of social capital, as developed by Robert Putnam, was influential on policy in welfare and community development. Putnam argued in his book, *Bowling Alone* (2000), that in the USA there had been a serious decline in community participation over the previous half century and that there was serious and increasing shortfall in stocks of social capital. This resonates with what many commentators and some studies by social scientists have observed in respect of British society. Putnam understands social capital as a good thing, and he defines and attempts to measure it largely as a property of communities and whole societies. More recently he has refined the concept by distinguishing bonding (within a community), bridging (across different communities) and linking (socially vertical) forms. He has also carried out major studies of the role of churches and other religious groups in providing the social glue for American society (published with David Campbell in 2010 as *American Grace*).

There are, of course, some critical voices in the debates who introduce modified concepts and theories (Bourdieu, 1986), while others dismiss the concept as meaningless. Unlike Putnam, Bourdieu sees social capital as an abstract property acquired by individuals or groups or networks of individuals, which can be used to competitive advantage in securing economic resources, status and power. Bourdieu also considers other forms of capital, such as cultural, human and religious capitals.

In my view, although social capital is poorly defined and intrinsically impossible to measure, the concept does have value as a useful metaphor, which has a resonance with popular debates about contemporary communities. However, in the context of the dominance of global market economics and their application to welfare services, it does seem significant, if not a little disturbing, that relationships in the community, based on Putnam's trinity of 'trust, networks and norms' and the Christian virtues of altruism, mutuality and solidarity with the marginalised, have been transformed using the language and metaphor of 'capital'.

In public policy terms, the usual argument based on Putnam is that voluntary action within civil society increases the stock of social capital and is to be regarded as a public good. Faith communities, particularly those in ethnically and religiously diverse urban areas, are recognised as banks of social capital which could, as it were, be invested for the public good in areas such as urban regeneration, social welfare and, especially after September 2001, in community cohesion and national security. Since 2010, under the coalition government headed by David Cameron, the notion of the 'Big Society' has been much in vogue. Under successive governments, voluntary groups, including faith-based congregations and charities, have been urged to play a more significant role in community work and social welfare, and the 'volunteer' is portrayed as the archetypal good citizen. Debates continue as to whether this offers a genuine space for religion to make a contribution in the public sphere or whether it is the state seeking to control and exploit the voluntary and faith sectors, in part as a cynical cost-cutting exercise.

In recent work at the William Temple Foundation, Chris Baker and other colleagues, including myself, have been widening the debate by developing theories of religious and spiritual capital. These forms of capital are seen as distinct but complementary dimensions to the well-established concept of social capital (in its various bonding, bridging and linking modes). In particular, we propose that *spiritual capital* in individuals comprises a theological or spiritual worldview, values and vision for the future, expressed in and mediated by activities such as prayer and worship. It is this that motivates a believer to make a practical and generous contribution to society. Such generosity is often located and mediated in a context of significant *religious capital*. We use this term to describe the practical contribution that faith groups (as institutions) make to society through the use of a building, volunteers, paid community workers, faith-based social networks and activities for particular age or interest groups.

What seems to be rarely discussed, however, is the concept of the labour or work that goes into the formation of social (or other forms of) capital. Yet it is clear to anyone who has a passing acquaintance with local churches that church members expend huge amounts of effort and energy on behalf of the religious organisation to which they belong. This may consist of practical physical labour devoted to the maintenance of a place of worship; religious labour aimed at sustaining and improving the programme of collective religious activities (through preaching, teaching, musical ministry, church administration, for example); or spiritual labour focused on developing personal growth (through prayer, Bible study and other spiritual disciplines). But there is also social labour, some of which is directed internally in the organisation (through spending time building fellowship, caring for one another and resolving conflict in the church), and some which is outward facing to the wider community – for example, through church community development programmes; through caring pastoral work with neighbours; and through the commitment of believers to paid and unpaid roles in schools, hospitals, voluntary organisations, community groups and local politics. Recently there was evidence of significant involvement by churches in community clean-up operations following the disturbances and frenzy of arson, criminal damage and looting in several English cities in August 2011.

Whatever stance one takes on the political debates around the Big Society, and however cynical one may be about the government's cost-cutting agenda, it is clear that the voluntary and constructive involvement of people in the life of their local community is a well-established feature of the life and values of Christian people. There is a sense in which churches have been labouring in pursuit of the Big Society long before the term was invented. Recognising this, the Evangelical Alliance has sought to support and strengthen such involvement, under the slogan 'Big Society – Kingdom Opportunity'. This is not to endorse any thought that the political programme of any government is identical or even congruent with the priorities of the kingdom of God. Indeed, there are times and issues where a critical and prophetic role of speaking truth to power is required. However, there are opportunities for Christian mission through these forms of community involvement. More fundamentally, in an imperfect society which bears all the scars of human sinfulness, there is an ongoing Christian duty to care for neighbours, to seek to do good and to work for the peace and welfare of the communities in which we live. And in a period where inequality and discontent appear to be growing, where common moral values are hard to find, and where the state and society as a whole seems reluctant to finance many of the aspects of welfare that were established in the second half of the twentieth century, the call to be involved in these ways appears stronger than ever.

The purpose of this chapter, then, is to look at the research evidence about these forms of social involvement, with particular reference to evangelical Christians. What is the extent and nature of their contribution through their social labour to the stock of social capital across the UK? Is there anything distinctive about it in comparison with the contribution of the general population, or with that of other forms of Christianity or other faith communities?

Faith that works: what the baseline survey reveals

In the baseline survey, the five main questions about volunteering were:

- How often do you:
  - > work as a volunteer for your church in an activity that serves the local community?
  - > work as a volunteer for a Christian organisation?
  - > work as a volunteer for a non-Christian organisation?
- Typically, how many hours a week do you volunteer in activities that serve/benefit the local community, and not just your church?
- (How much do you agree that) it is a Christian's duty to volunteer in activities that serve the local community?

There are, perhaps inevitably, some questions about the interpretation of these questions by respondents. In particular, different people could have different understandings of the term 'serves the local community': some may believe intercessory prayer does this just as much as feeding the homeless. However, the intention behind, and most likely interpretation of, this term is to focus on externally directed labour that builds broad social capital, rather than church-directed work that enhances religious and spiritual capital.

The headline finding is that 81% of evangelical Christians do some form of voluntary work serving the wider community with their church at least once a year, and 37% do so at least once a week.

There is an almost universal norm or aspiration of involvement and service among evangelicals. Of the evangelical respondents, 87% are in agreement (30% 'agree' and 57% 'strongly agree') that, 'It is a Christian's duty to volunteer in activities that serve the local community.' This norm is expressed in statements such as these:

> To be the hands and feet of Jesus in a needy world. To show the love of Christ by my life lived and witness, and to see the need of a hurting lost people and do what I can to meet that need with God's help.

> To love and serve unconditionally – showing the love of God by acts of kindness and neighbourliness, 'preaching the gospel without words'.

> To be salt and light where God has placed you, at home, work, school or leisure.

Graph 3.1 shows volunteering rates from the 12,593 respondents in the survey who defined themselves as evangelical Christians. The overall picture is clear:

- More than 80% of evangelical respondents say they volunteer at least once a year in a church activity serving the community, and more than 37% do this at least once every week. The corresponding figures on this question for 3,595 non-evangelical Christians in the survey were 70% and 26%, and for the 920 self-defined non-Christians (clearly they were in some way involved in churches and their wider networks in order to do so), 60% and 24%.

- A total of 52% respondents say they volunteer for a Christian organisation at least once a year, and about 21% do this at least once every week. It is interesting that more people who 'work daily' do so for a Christian organisation rather than for their church, suggesting that they are more or less full-time volunteers – for example, on a gap year or in retirement. The corresponding figures on this question for non-evangelical Christians in the survey were 40% and 14.5%, and for the non-Christians, 38% and 14%.

- Approximately 32% say they volunteer for a non-Christian organisation at least once a year, and about 11% do this at least once every week. The corresponding figures on this question for non-evangelical Christians in the survey were 33% and 12%, and for the non–Christians, 31% and 10%. The differences in volunteering rates for secular organisations between evangelicals and others are not significant, which seems to suggest that almost all the additional volunteering by evangelicals can be accounted for by their deeper involvement in active churches and the world of explicitly Christian organisations around them.

- While two-thirds of the evangelical respondents spend some unpaid time serving the community in some way, 50% offer four hours or fewer each week, while fewer than one in ten offers seven or more hours (see table 3.1).

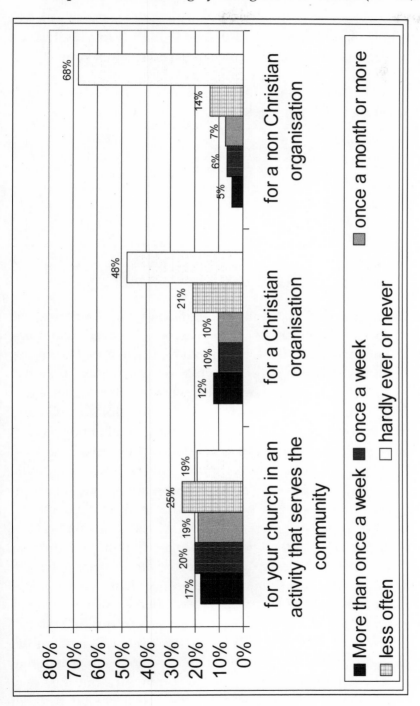

Graph 3.1 Volunteering by evangelical Christians (N = 12,953)

Table 3.1 Hours given (Baseline survey: evangelicals only)

Typically, how many hours a week do you volunteer in activities that serve/benefit the local community, and not just your church?	
Volunteering hours per week	**Per cent**
none	33%
2 or fewer	32%
3 or 4	19%
5 or 6	6%
7 or 8	3%
9 or more	6%
Total (N= 12,593)	100%

These figures suggest that a highly significant contribution to the welfare of society is made by evangelicals. However, they also highlight the importance of the local church as a base for evangelicals' unpaid labour. Perhaps this is because it is the place where they feel most comfortable and aligned with the ethos of the organisation; perhaps it is because the church presents multiple needs and opportunities for volunteers that are easy to engage with. Perhaps also, as the most significant community of interest in their lives, the local church fellowship shares a strong implicit norm towards internal volunteering, or sometimes subtle (or perhaps not so subtle) moral pressure by asking for people 'to help out in this important ministry'.

The statistics also suggest that while the contribution of evangelicals to the work of the wider or secular voluntary sector is far from negligible, it remains the case that they favour or prioritise work where religious values are shared and more explicitly expressed. It may well be a consequence of a theology of holiness which involves separation from the wider world which is seen as intrinsically sinful. Such patterns of involvement are likely to strengthen religious capital in churches and Christian organisations and promote strong bonding forms of social capital within the Christian community. But they may restrict the growth of bridging and linking social capital through weaker but fruitful links with people and institutions that are different from themselves. As one respondent said:

> Much of our 'Christian service' is locked into church activities when there is so much opportunity outside of that arena for Christians to be a positive presence.

We can therefore pose the question whether this tendency to remain within the 'cocoon' of the Christian world gives a negative impression to outsiders and to some extent limits the potential influence of evangelicals in society at large, including the potential for evangelism through strong and extensive community networks.

Comparison with the wider population

While more than 80% of the evangelicals in our survey say they do some voluntary service at least once a year, respondents who do not define themselves as evangelicals show statistically significant lower rates of volunteering. (For example, only 70% of those who say they are Christian but not evangelical and only 60% of those who do not claim to be Christians do any such work.) This compares with a baseline figure for the general population, as reported from the 2007 government *Citizenship Survey*, of 39.2% who were involved in formal volunteering in the previous 12 months. (For a more detailed analysis of more recent citizenship survey data on religion and social involvement, see Birdwell & Littler, 2012).

A superficial analysis of these citizenship surveys suggests that respondents who are practising Jewish, Christian, Buddhist or of no religion are more likely than average to be involved in formal volunteering, while Hindus, Sikhs and Muslims are less likely than average to be involved in this way. However, after some complex statistical analysis (involving logistical regression techniques) on an early wave of the *Citizenship Survey*, the key conclusions reported in a conference paper I gave in 2006 were:

> Religious affiliation as such appears to have no significant effect on volunteering rates when class-related variables, ethnicity, age, gender and variables relating to integration into the local neighbourhood are taken into account. However, those who report their religious identity as important or who

Graph 3.2 Formal volunteering in last 12 months from 2007 *Citizenship Survey*

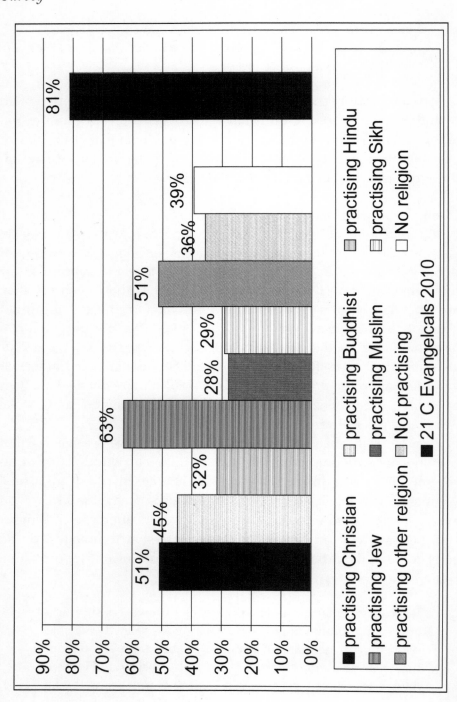

have been recent or regular attenders at worship are significantly more likely to report formal volunteering in a group context. This effect is particularly noticeable among Christians.

Our data suggests that in terms of volunteering rates, evangelicals are the extreme case for practising Christians and do indeed volunteer more than any other religious group in the population.

Who volunteers most among evangelicals?

In order to clarify which types of evangelical Christians are most likely to serve the community as volunteers, we ran cross tabulations of the three questions about volunteering (with categories combined and simplified) and the attitude statement about it being a Christian duty, against demographic factors such as gender, age, household income, membership of a black majority church. We also looked at the effect of spiritual capital variables such as (self-reported) daily prayer and Bible reading. The analysis is too detailed to be presented here in full, but here are some of the key findings.

Gender
For volunteering within a church or secular context, women are more likely than men to be regularly involved.

Age
The chances of being a regular volunteer are greatest for the 65–74 age group, and lowest for the 35–44 age group, who are much more likely to be under time pressure through employment and raising families.

Income
Broadly speaking, wealthier respondents are less likely than those of modest means to give unpaid labour to serve the community. This may be because retired people and others with time on their hands are less likely to have large incomes.

Type of church

Black majority church (BMC) members are less likely than average to be regularly serving the community through their church. However, they are more likely than average to volunteer for a Christian organisation (only 42% said they rarely or never do so, compared with 48% overall). On the other hand, more than 75% of BMC members strongly agree that such service is a Christian's duty – well above the overall average of 56%.

This is quite a complex pattern of difference, and it would be dangerous to draw too many conclusions other than that there are different cultural and theological norms about the relationship of church and society and different demographic and employment patterns which may limit availability for voluntary work among BMC members.

Spiritual capital

Around 46% of those who pray daily and 48% of those who read the Bible daily serve at least fortnightly, compared with the average of 43%. Similar statistically significant differences could be seen for volunteering in Christian organisations and on the attitude statement. However, for regular volunteering in secular organisations, the differences are very small.

These figures would suggest that higher levels of spiritual capital are associated with a greater propensity to serve, but they may also tend to keep people's active involvement within the Christian subculture, or be linked to age factors in that retired people report both greater rates of volunteering and spending more time in prayer and Bible reading.

Multiple volunteering

Of the respondents who volunteer at least weekly in a church activity serving the wider community:

* 39% also volunteer at least weekly for a Christian organisation, 29% less often and 32% never;

* 16% also volunteer at least weekly for a secular organisation, 23% less often and 60% never.

These extremely active multiple volunteers are more likely than non-volunteers to report weekly or greater church attendance, daily personal prayer and daily Bible reading. They are also more likely to be female, to be in their fifties or sixties, and to be in the lower income bands.

There are, of course, some correlations between the variables we have examined – for example, over-65s are likely to have a lower income, and are more likely to be females (as men on average experience failing health and death at an earlier stage). Older people may also have more time and a cultural/religious background which favours more disciplined spirituality (the 'Quiet Time' generation). The black community, on the other hand, is known to have a younger age profile than average.

An initial exploration with some multiple regression analysis suggests that variables based on spiritual capital indicators play the most important part in predicting who will be an active volunteer, that age and lower income also have a significant effect, and that gender and belonging to a black majority church play little part in the equation. There is evidence therefore to support the suggestion that the higher a person's spiritual capital, or the more zealous they are in their faith, as they reach mature years, and provided they are not in the higher income brackets, the more likely they are to give substantial amounts of time and unpaid labour in serving their community.

Involvement in public life: evidence from the *Does belief touch society?* panel survey

In the online panel survey conducted over the Easter period in 2011, a total of 1,151 respondents answered a battery of questions about faith and practice, including a section relating to the overall theme of social capital and civic involvement.

We wanted to gather more information about the engagement of Christians in society so asked people whether they were involved in various areas of public life. No one among our sample was (or admitted to being) a member of Parliament. However, nearly 1% said they were local councillors (compared to 0.04% nationally), and 0.78% were magistrates (compared to 0.06% nationally). Among the councillors and magistrates, it was significant that none was under 35.

An amazing 24.5% (282 people) said they were trustees of charities (compared to 2.2% nationally. Detailed analysis of supplementary information, where given, shows that a significant proportion (62 people) were able to say they were charity trustees by virtue of the fact that they were on church councils or the equivalent. Nonetheless, respondents held many trustee positions (in 21 cases more than one) in both Christian (65) and secular-based (36) charities. Charity trustees were significantly more likely to be university educated and over the age of 55, and twice as likely to be men than women. Pentecostals and our category of miscellaneous 'other' Protestant denominations were less likely than average to serve in these roles than, for example, Anglicans, Methodists, Baptists and members of 'new' charismatic churches.

More than 100 people in the sample (nearly 9%) were school governors (compared to 0.7% nationally). School governors were significantly more likely to be over the age of 35, male and from Anglican and Methodist backgrounds.

Nearly 4% were members of a political party (compared to 1.3% nationally). Members of political parties were four times more likely to be male (8% of respondents) than female (2%). Of those who declared their allegiance, ten were Labour, five Liberal Democrat, three Conservative, two SNP and one Plaid Cymru.

In contrast, trade union membership stood at 18.5% – a figure that is roughly the same as national membership for the working age population. However, as our sample contained many retired and non-employed people, the proportion was actually much higher than average. The most frequently named trade union was Unison (37), followed by NUT (21), NASUWT (18), UNITE (12), RCN (10) and ATL (10). This suggests a strong representation in the educational, health and general public services sectors, which tend to be more highly unionised. While a number of trade unionists expressed reluctance about their membership and stressed they were not militant, an almost equal number said they were stewards or local officers in their unions. In our *Working faithfully?* survey in May 2013, about 35% said they had been a union member during their working life and 4% that they had been active in it, while 6% had been unhappy with the way it operated. Another 16% had been a member of a staff association or professional body rather than a union. A further 7% said it was against their principles to join a trade union.

While the nature of the sample and the online method of carrying out this research may have over-represented people who are more likely to be active in the public sphere, the results represent a huge investment of unpaid time and energy by evangelical Christians in the voluntary and community sector, in education and health services, in politics and in the trade union movement. This is to a large extent in addition to the work they undertake in their paid employment and in the life of their local church.

Are we good neighbours? survey 2014

Our February 2014 panel survey involved 1,497 evangelical Christians who answered a range of questions about their interactions with neighbours and involvement in community life in the neighbourhoods where they lived.

A total of 59% of respondents said they are involved actively in at least one church social action or community outreach project. However, only 21% are actively involved in any secular project or activity, among which, work with people with disabilities or learning difficulties is the most common.

Many of our respondents are involved in numerous social action projects. The mean average number of church projects or activities (including the 41% who are not involved in any) is 1.57. Church leaders are often involved in many projects (their average is 2.6). Men are more likely to be involved in multiple projects than women, and younger women are least likely to be involved in church projects (women born after 1980 scored only 0.76). However, when controlled for the likelihood that church leaders tend to be older men, it becomes clear that a church leadership role is the best predictor of multiple involvement, and that age plays a part as older people do more activities, with some effect from being involved in a large church (which might better sustain multiple activities).

The data also shows that people are in churches where overseas linked projects are most popular, followed by foodbanks, care for the elderly, families and youth outreach.

According to the Home Office *Citizenship Survey 2003*, 42% of people socialise with their neighbours or friends at least once a week, and another 25% at least once a month.'

Our data from the panel suggests that about two-thirds have casual conversations with neighbours each week, though maybe only around a quarter are willing to go into each other's homes. It is not possible to make a direct comparison with the citizenship survey data here because of the different phrasing of questions, though it would seem fair to say our evangelicals are at least as sociable with their neighbours as anyone else in the population, perhaps more.

In terms of local involvement and concern for people in the local community, our panel survey shows a mixed picture. About a third have a prayer concern for their community; a quarter help lonely, frail or needy neighbours on a regular basis or look to welcome newcomers. The rates reported for supporting schools and for participating in residents groups and hobby interest groups suggest a higher than average level of social involvement in communities. Participation in sports groups and socialising at the pub can seem low, but this can probably be explained by the age profile of the panel and the traditional temperance culture of evangelicals which keeps them distant from the drinking culture found in many communities.

Graph 3.3 Social project involvement: *Are we good neighbours?* survey (N = 1,497 evangelicals)

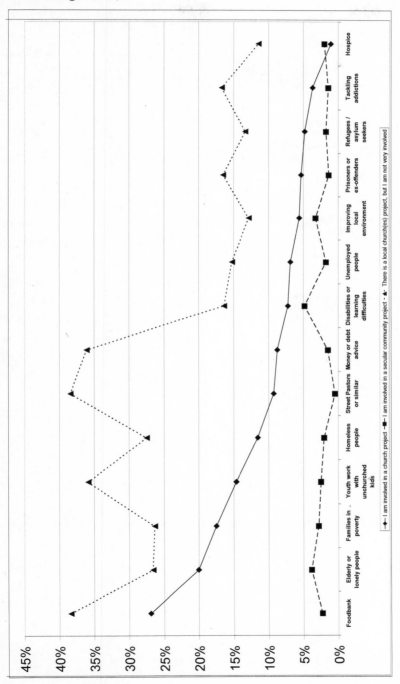

Graph 3.4 Your neighbours. When did you last ...? *Are we good neighbours?* survey (N = 1,497 evangelicals)

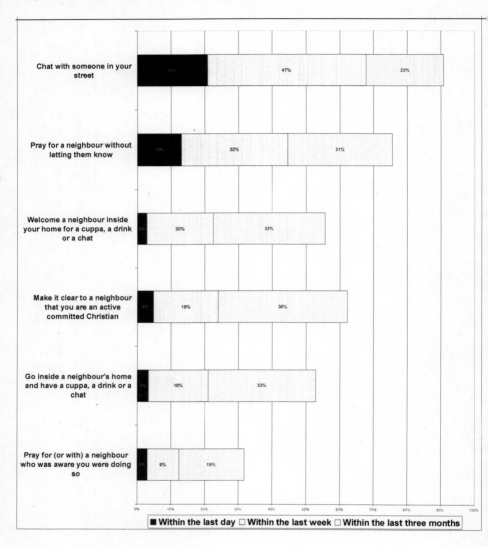

Graph 3.5 Local involvement: *Are we good neighbours?* survey (N = 1,497 evangelicals)

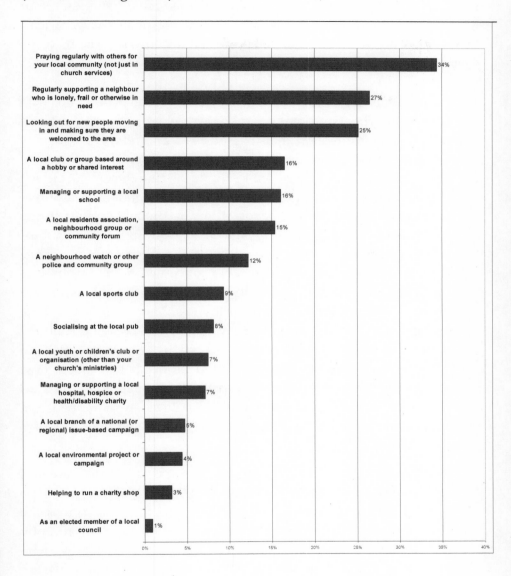

Conclusions and further questions

First of all, the evidence presented in this paper suggests four remarkable things about evangelical Christians (or at the very least about the kind of evangelicals who are willing to take part in social surveys like ours):

1. Evangelicals are in comparison with the general population, with Christians who would not describe themselves as evangelical, and with people from most other religious backgrounds. They are very socially active and politically engaged. They have high levels of social capital in bonding within the local church and in linking between the rich and the poor, which can often mobilise resources for mission and charitable action. They are probably not so strong in terms of bridging social capital or in working in partnerships which take them outside the evangelical faith community. They tend to be active citizens, charitably concerned for the welfare of the whole community, and willing to contribute time, skills and energy within their church activities and beyond. These evangelicals certainly cannot be accused of withdrawing from the world but have taken seriously the call to be salt and light in wider society. Further research would be needed to assess how effectively they undertake such tasks, the issues and problems they face in these roles, and how well they are equipped and supported theologically and practically by the churches to which they belong.

2. Demographic biases in our samples of respondents may account for some of this high level of engagement, as a disproportionate number of evangelicals (in our sample and probably across the churches) are educated middle class, middle aged or recently retired. These are the very groups in generic official surveys who have been found to be most likely to volunteer. However, we are unable to use demographics to explain everything, and when other variables are controlled, we can detect little to suggest gender or ethnic differences in the propensity to volunteer.

3. These evangelicals also show high levels of spiritual capital, measured in strong commitment to orthodox Christian beliefs and

moral values, in high reported levels of church attendance, and in personal practice of Scripture reading and prayer. They appear pious yet are in no way 'so heavenly minded that they are of no earthly use'.

4. There does appear to be a measurable positive relationship between spiritual capital and offering unpaid labour to enhance society's storehouse of social capital. It is the most zealous of the evangelicals, whose religious practice appears most faithful, who are most likely to give their time in serving others.

A number of questions arise, on which evangelicals and their leaders would do well to reflect as the church becomes more involved in social and community action and debates about it in the public sphere:

1. How far are evangelicals constrained in their social action by the 'cocoon' of their own church or the Christian subculture? There is some evidence in our findings that the respondents are more willing to work within church settings than for secular organisations delivering valuable social interventions. Is it the case that the involvement of evangelicals in the 'world' demands a framework of religious and social capital that provides a degree of separation (holiness), or is this in fact detrimental to successful outcomes in mission?

2. Is the motivation for evangelical Christians to do 'good works' mainly driven by social factors associated with belonging to a church where such activity is the norm? Or are the spiritual capital factors of prayer, Bible study, firm doctrinal belief and the practice of regular worship the critical factors in promoting activism?

3. Are evangelical Christians naive in the way they offer their contribution to the welfare of society? In particular, in the present economic and social climate surrounded by the somewhat vague language of the 'Big Society', are Christians, by providing free social labour, colluding with a government that is by its policies producing greater levels of poverty, inequality and injustice that contradict the values of the kingdom of God? Are they stuck in a

model of simply providing charitable assistance to people in need, or are they willing and able to use community development and partnership models to empower people in mutual support and self-determination, giving them a voice in the public realm, even if they are not (yet) Christian believers? What is the right balance between charity and care on the one hand and prophecy and protest on the other?

4. Are evangelicals purely altruistic in their commitment, or do they serve with the explicit or implicit aim of sharing the gospel and recruiting new members to their churches? Are they in fact seeking a reward, which might be simply feeling good about themselves or (despite their belief in already being justified by faith) still seeking approval from God?

5. If the highest levels of active volunteering come from the late middle aged and active seniors generation, what is going to happen in coming decades? If active membership in churches and the vitality of Christian faith communities is in decline while the economic and time pressures on younger people increase, what is going to become of all the activities and programmes that are currently being sustained by evangelical Christian volunteers? Strong secularisation theory is predicting the inexorable decline of Christian influence in the UK, while weaker formulations suggest that believing without belonging, spirituality without organised religion, will persist. If either of these are correct, then is it also the case that positive activity to enhance social capital and work for the welfare of communities and those in need will also decline?

6. If such a useful contribution to the welfare of society is to be sustained in the medium to long term, how much does this depend on the successful outcome of an evangelical mission where proclamation of the faith, persuasion of unbelievers, recruitment of new church members, and effective discipleship programmes form people as social activists? One might argue that society as a whole, just as much as the church, needs effective evangelism if we wish to see humanity flourish.

References

Baker, C. & Smith, G (2011). 'Spiritual, religious and social capital – exploring their dimensions and their relationship with faith-based motivation and participation in UK civil society.' Summary working paper Manchester: William Temple Foundation (Based on a paper presented at the BSA Sociology of Religion Group Conference, Edinburgh April 2010). Available at http://williamtemplefoundation.org.uk/wp-content/uploads/2014/03/Spiritual-Religious-Social-Capital-Baker-Smith.pdf (accessed 21st August 2014).

Birdwell, Jonathan & Littler, Mark (2012). 'Why those who do God, do good...' Faithful Citizens © Demos. Some rights reserved. Magdalen House, 136 Tooley Street, London, SE1 2TU.

Bourdieu, P. (1986). 'The Forms of Capital'. In J. G . Richardson (ed.). *Handbook for Theory and Research for the Sociology of Education*. New York: Greenwood Press: 241–58.

Putnam, Robert D (2000). *Bowling Alone: The Collapse and Revival of American Community*. New York: Simon & Schuster, 2000.

Putnam, Robert D. & Campbell, David E. *American Grace: How Religion Divides and Unites Us*. New York: Simon & Schuster.

Smith, G, (2006). 'Faith, Volunteering and Social Capital: What the Surveys Say'. Paper presented at NCVO Research Conference, University of Warwick, September 2006.

Response to chapter 3

Fran Beckett OBE

The findings outlined in this fascinating and in many ways heartening chapter will inevitably leave the reader with many questions, not least the excellent ones at the end.

There are some important contextual considerations that need mentioning. In our post-Christendom twenty-first century world, the church is being increasingly pushed to the margins of society, although our plugging of gaps caused by public finance cuts has helped our credibility. Also significant are postmodern attitudes illustrated in the growing mistrust of institutions, including the church.

Consequently, some evangelicals have sought to respond by developing culturally relevant or new, simpler models of church, what Archbishop Rowan Williams called 'a mixed economy of church'. Each has a distinct approach and level of priority given to social action. Examples include incarnational missional communities embedded in neighbourhoods, concentrating on being with people in their situations, and pursuing small-scale relational rather than project interventions. The new monastic movement's focus on generosity, simplicity and hospitality again reflects a highly relational rather than a project approach. 'Messy church', focusing on children and families, brings with it the possibility of family support activities. More outward-looking 'emerging' churches concentrate on supporting their members to be missional salt and light Christians in all areas of life rather than upon collective church social action. And cyber church arguably has little to do with encouraging volunteering or Christian social action.

The latter years of the twentieth century saw growing acceptance by evangelicals of caring action being part of the church's mission. However, the survey indicates that social justice, which tackles the institutional causes of social need, is still a poor relation. For example, volunteering in foodbanks features strongly in the survey results and, while this undoubtedly makes a real difference in people's lives, there is a troubling question about how far they are inadvertently helping politicians to ignore the unintended consequences of recent welfare reform. Is it enough to celebrate the substantial amount of social action activity by evangelicals, which indeed we should, or do we also need to face some searching questions about the implications of where our energies are focused?

With less external funding available for churches, will they be willing to divert resources from 'internal' activities? What will the answer to this say about our mission priorities?

We are told that those most likely to volunteer are in the 65–74 age group. As these people age, and as many of the baby boomer generation don't formally retire, opting instead for gradually reducing their paid employment, the church will struggle to maintain this current level of volunteering. Tackling this impending resource gap will necessitate teaching and discipling that focuses on the second half of life being 'lived well' and rebuts negative attitudes to ageing. It will also have implications for the discipling of younger Christians and our expectations of what church involvement means.

There is much to be encouraged by here, but in the midst of our loving action we should also be those who seek to understand the times and know what we should do (1 Chronicles 12:32).

Fran Beckett OBE is formerly the CEO of the Shaftesbury Society and Church Urban Fund. She now combines Christian community involvement in Peckham with charity consultancy, leadership mentoring, speaking and writing.

Chapter 4: Evangelicalism and politics

Mathew Guest

It would be fair to characterise the current political climate of the UK –
at least in comparison with its recent history – as somewhat unstable.
A series of scandals concerning expenses claims has eroded public
trust in politicians, while widespread disillusionment with the
electoral process is reflected in poor voter turnouts at local and
national level. The proportion of the electorate who are members of
the mainstream political parties is the lowest it has been since the early
1980s.

At the same time, the party political map of the country has been
changing. Following 13 years of government under New Labour, for
the most part coinciding with a period of economic boom, 2010 saw
the first general election resulting in no overall majority since 1974. A
coalition government of Conservatives and Liberal Democrats
grappling with the challenges of the economic downturn brought
mixed fortunes for both parties, with many traditional Lib Dem
supporters particularly disillusioned with a party they perceived as
having overly compromised to Tory policies. Labour, in the meantime,
did not experience the resurgence in popularity many hoped for. All
this makes the outcome of the 2015 general election hard to predict.

There is a sense that the parameters of the past are giving way to a
new kind of politics, and yet the uncertainty as to what this means
generates understandable anxieties among politicians, media
commentators and the public at large. While party-political support
appears to be at an all-time low, continued trade union action against
public sector job cuts and pay freezes, as well as energetic
campaigning by organisations like UK Uncut and the Global Occupy
movement, suggest that large groups of people are channelling their
political views in ways aside from the ballot box.

A very different kind of movement is presented when one considers
the rise of the UK Independence Party (UKIP) in recent years. From
minority special interest group to the UK's 'fourth party', UKIP has
secured seats in the European Parliament and on local councils and, as
of October 2014, has its first Member of Parliament in Tory-defector

Douglas Carswell. UKIP's success coincides with an upsurge in support for right-wing nationalist parties in other parts of continental Europe, signalling grassroots scepticism about the European Union and provoking anxieties about associated perspectives on immigration and cultural diversity.

Recent years have also seen interesting developments in the ways in which Christian churches relate to the political process. The traditional image of the Church of England as the 'Tory Party at Prayer' was finally demolished in the 1980s, when influential figures in the established church openly opposed the Conservative government's policies on a range of issues, from the handling of the Falklands War to the implications of free market economics for the inner-city poor. Instrumental in addressing the latter was Bishop of Liverpool David Sheppard, who was also a key figure behind the 'Faith in the City' report published in 1985. Sheppard is especially relevant here because he was both an influential bishop in the Church of England and a fervent evangelical, a firm advocate of evangelical theology and an equally passionate campaigner on behalf of the poor and disenfranchised in British society.

Subsequent years have found evangelicals shifting their public self-expression between maintaining a traditional focus on individual salvation – as with the so-called 'decade of evangelism' in the 1990s – and affirming an interventionist voice speaking truth to power in the public square. Such interventions have responded both to matters of individual rights and freedoms – as with legal cases involving Christians apparently penalised for expressing their faith in the workplace – and to issues of structural immorality, such as the plight of economically deprived groups exploited by 'payday loans' companies. The form of such intervention has also varied, from direct lobbying at the heart of Westminster to the issuing of church-sponsored reports, to public campaigning involving protest marches, and increasing use of social media. Evangelicals rarely speak with a united voice in these circumstances, and campaign organisations have tended each to focus their resources on a particular set of issues: gender roles and church leadership for Reform; the legal challenging of discrimination against Christians for The Christian Legal Centre; the moral decline of Britain for The Christian Institute; poverty and disease in the developing world for Tearfund.

While these various issues have become the focus of well-resourced and concerted campaigning from evangelical organisations, it is unclear how grassroots evangelical Christians engage with the broader political process. What kinds of issues are they most concerned about? To which kinds of campaign do they commit most resources? And how do their doctrinal and ethical priorities translate into political action? The data gathered from our surveys allows these questions to be pursued from a fresh evidence base, and some of the emerging trends are explored in the present chapter.

Engagement in the political process

When asked what the priorities of the Evangelical Alliance should be, respondents to the Omnibus Survey (administered August 2013, internally reported only) were given a number of options, from 'Bringing together local churches/church leaders' to 'Providing theological leadership to the evangelical community' and 'Mobilising the church locally and nationally for mission', among others. Notably, the option with the highest proportion of respondents affirming it as a 'top priority' was 'Representing the evangelical community to government and media'. A total of 53% answered in this way, compared with 31% who accorded 'top priority' status to 'Mobilising the church locally and nationally for mission', and 19% who did so for 'Providing theological leadership to the evangelical community'. Moreover, only 1% of respondents felt that representing evangelicals to government and media was an 'inappropriate' role for the EA, suggesting that support for an apolitical evangelicalism – focused exclusively on matters of personal faith – is much lower than it once was. In a striking finding from our 2010 survey, 91.9% of evangelical respondents agreed that it is important for Christians to engage with government, national assemblies and parliament (more than 75% agreeing 'a lot'). So there is an enthusiasm among the majority for a politically engaged evangelicalism, and for the Evangelical Alliance having a role in promoting the values of evangelicalism within the public sphere, including among politicians. But what do they see this as meaning in practical terms?

The most obvious place to look for evidence of political activity among evangelicals is their participation in the electoral process. Our 2010 survey, following the UK's general election, found that a large majority of respondents – 80.1% – had voted, well in excess of the 65.1% national turnout. Among those affirming an evangelical identity, this rises to 84.7%, suggesting that an evangelical commitment may coincide with a greater tendency to engage with the electoral process.

However, this has to be considered in light of the demographic constituency of our respondents, who are disproportionately middle to upper-middle class and middle aged to elderly, and include a higher proportion of men than the national population. According to data collected by Ipsos MORI based on the 2010 general election results, all of these factors are associated with a stronger tendency to vote. This suggests we should not be surprised that our respondents appear especially well motivated, as this may have more to do with their social class, age and gender distribution than their evangelical commitment.

Nevertheless, there are signs that our respondents may well exceed patterns within the general population when it comes to engaging with the political processes of the UK. In our Easter 2011 survey, 91% said they would be voting in the imminent Referendum on the alternative vote, around double the national turnout on the day. Around 4% said they are members of a political party (compared to 1.3% nationally), and 1% are local councillors (compared to the much lower national proportion of 0.04%). Moreover, in the 2011 *Are we communicating?* survey, respondents were asked whether they had raised a concern in the political or public sphere during the previous 12 months using a variety of methods. In response, 51.9% said they have emailed their MP, local councillor or other politician; 70.9% have signed a petition on paper (80.7% have signed one online); 57% have used online media to forward campaign information; and 29% have actually met their MP or other politician to talk to them directly.

Respondents to the same survey were asked about times when they have been asked by an organisation or charity other than their own church during the previous 12 months to do something – perhaps to donate money, to undertake a volunteering role or to take part in a campaign to influence government (UK or overseas). Significantly more have been asked to donate money to a charitable cause or Christian charity than have been approached about volunteering or campaigning. However, when asked whether they agreed to do what was asked of them, political campaigning secured a higher rate of committed responses than volunteering and donating money. Of those asked to take part in political campaigning during the previous 12 months, 81.4% had agreed to do this (compared to 70% of those asked to volunteer and 79% of those asked to make a donation). Political action is apparently not shied away from by our evangelical respondents.

Support for political parties

It is possible to build a picture of the party political profile of our respondents by examining data on voting preferences drawn from the 2010 baseline survey. These combine the results from a pre-election survey about voting intentions with post-election surveys of other evangelical populations about how they actually voted. Taking these together and comparing them with the actual general election results, we can discern just how distinctive evangelical respondents are from the national population.

The data suggests that evangelical respondents are more likely than the general population to favour the Conservative Party, but only by 3.3 percentage points. It also suggests that they are more likely to favour the Liberal Democrats (by 6.1 percentage points) and less likely to support Labour (by 6.9 percentage points). Interestingly, support for Labour among evangelicals attending black majority churches is much higher, at 61%. In explaining this, it is tempting to cite long-rehearsed arguments that refer to the special appeal of Pentecostalism among the working classes and the poor, although recent research into British Pentecostalism within black majority churches suggests a more complex demographic constituency, including many among the aspirant middle classes (Hunt and Lightly, 2001). Moreover, according to the Ethnic Minority British Election Study, based on survey data collected after the 2010 election, around seven in every ten ethnic minority Britons are supportive of Labour irrespective of their social class status (Heath & Khan, 2012).

The same survey reveals a persistent concern among ethnic minorities about equal opportunities in society, although the fact that support for Labour, while high, is down from previous elections may suggest they have decreasing faith that the Labour Party can deliver on this issue. The still lower support among black majority church evangelicals in our survey could indicate an even more diminished perspective on the Labour Party. Indeed, the markedly entrepreneurial spirit of such churches – many of which have raised money from their communities for their own buildings and demand high levels of practical commitment from members – reflects values of self-sufficiency, innovation and individual effort most commonly associated with the Conservatives. Admittedly, following Tony Blair's New Labour, the Tories can no longer be claimed as the only party in full support of economic enterprise.

It is unclear to what extent black evangelicals make a positive connection between their entrepreneurial spirit and the economic message of the Conservative Party. So far there seems little evidence that this is the case, whether because Labour have absorbed those associations or because associations between Labour and social justice remain paramount in their political decision making.

Among our evangelical respondents, differences from the national electorate in support of minor parties were often smaller (for example, the Green Party secured support from 1% of the national population and from 1.2% of our responding evangelicals, while UKIP achieved 3.1% of the national vote and support from 1% of evangelicals). Interestingly, only 1.1% of our respondents expressed support for Christian political parties (such as the Christian Party or Christian People's Alliance). While this may suggest a very limited appetite for political representation by specifically 'Christian' parties in national government, it is worth bearing in mind that the option to vote for a 'Christian' party is by no means available in every constituency.

Given our rather transitional political climate, it is helpful to place such snapshot findings within a more longitudinal context. Do they represent a stable arrangement or are they changing over time? Respondents were asked about their intentions with respect to voting in a UK general election at two points: in 2010 and in 2013 within our *Working faithfully?* survey. Firstly, there was a sizeable proportion of 'I don't know' responses, suggesting a strong caution against any use of these figures in forecasting election results. However, the undecided 39.3% from 2010 had considerably shrunk by 2013, to 27.3%, perhaps indicating a firmer sense of alignment with specific parties in the approach to the 2015 general election. While acknowledging this proportion of undecided respondents, several interesting patterns can be observed in these figures with respect to support for the main political parties. Comparing the two points in time, support for the Conservative Party declines from 35.7% to 24.1% of respondents expressing a preference; Labour support increases from 23.1% to 27.3%; Liberal Democrat support decreases from 33.5% to 15.9%.

From one point of view, these figures are not surprising: one would expect the governing party to suffer declining support as we move further in time from their ascendency to power, and we can see both parties of the coalition government suffering from this mid-term dip. The Liberal Democrats appear to have suffered particularly badly, with their proportion of evangelical supporters more than halving over the three-year period. Correspondingly, the main party of opposition – Labour – received increasing support, just overtaking the Conservatives.

However, the most significant beneficiaries of disillusionment with the coalition government are the minor political parties. Among those expressing a party preference, support for the Green Party increased from 2% to 6%. Support for either the Christian People's Alliance or the Christian Party increased from 1.8% to 10.5% of respondents, suggesting a shift in willingness to consider seriously options outside of the three main parties, including those explicitly identifying themselves as Christian. UKIP appears to have benefited from the same kind of disillusionment with the Conservative, Labour and Liberal Democrat parties, although its recent increase in popularity has a more obvious place within broader debates, particularly those concerned with national identity and immigration. The shift to UKIP may be our most striking finding among evangelicals, securing support from 1.6% of our survey respondents in 2010, increasing to 13.2% in 2013 – a more than eight-fold increase, with evidence to suggest much stronger support among men than women. Furthermore, when respondents to our 2014 *Faith in politics?* survey were asked who among the current party leaders would make the most capable prime minister, 6.44% named Nigel Farage as their first choice, ahead of Nick Clegg who secured only 6.19%. It would seem that the national rise of UKIP as the 'fourth party' of British politics is reflected in a growing contingent of supporters among evangelical Christians.

UKIP and evangelical values

Ascertaining why UKIP might appeal to evangelical voters in increasing numbers is a difficult question to answer. However, some recent data collected in the summer of 2014 in a panel survey specifically concerned with politics offers some helpful clues. This survey included a number of questions about politics and political choices, including one about why individuals might have a different party preference compared to how they voted at the last election.

Those who find themselves disillusioned with the Tory Party mentioned one issue far more than any other: the introduction of the Marriage (Same Sex Couples) Act in 2013, which effectively made it possible for adults of the same sex to marry in a religious ceremony. Unsurprisingly, the majority of evangelicals appear firmly opposed to same-sex marriage: no fewer than 80% of our 2011 Easter survey respondents stated that the legal status of marriage should *not* be extended to include other relationships, including partnerships between same-sex couples. For many evangelical respondents, this is such a fundamental issue of Christian principle that, following the legal changes of 2013, they do not feel able to vote Conservative again. The same-sex marriage Act is an accommodation too far to the values of modern society for many who would otherwise have remained faithful Tory supporters. With this as a defining issue, it is not surprising that these same individuals did not shift allegiance to Labour or the Lib Dems, both of whom fully backed the 2013 bill. Within the context of this debate, for some evangelicals, UKIP has emerged as the party most supportive of the traditional view of marriage that they most fervently defend. As one respondent put it, 'UKIP is the only party that supports marriage.'

For some respondents, the perceived 'attack' on marriage by the three main parties is associated with an anti-Christian agenda, including opposition to the teaching of creationism in schools. Some even go a step further in characterising UKIP as the party of Christian values, such as the respondent who, echoing the words of Nigel Farage, commented that, 'Nobody except UKIP is coming anywhere near the problem of the UK forsaking its Judeo-Christian heritage.'

The issue of Europe was the second most cited reason for switching to UKIP, and our respondents include a significant number of Euro-sceptics who see the European Union as diverting resources from the

UK's interests, and/or as an organisation not to be trusted. One respondent went as far as to say, 'It is an institution set up with deceit and I would not trust it a millimetre, ever.' UKIP support also seems to be strongly associated with perspectives that connect immigration to the economic plight of the country. Our 2013 *Working faithfully?* survey revealed that those likely to vote UKIP are much more likely to agree that the government should reduce immigration in order to safeguard jobs for British workers (75.4%, compared to 31.9% of all other evangelical respondents).

However, it is important to note that, for those wholeheartedly embracing UKIP as their new party of choice, there are just as many making a careful differentiation between how they would vote in different kinds of election. For these respondents, UKIP would receive their vote in a European election – as a protest against the EU – but not in a general election. As one put it, 'UKIP have valuable things to consider regarding Europe and immigration, but not necessarily regarding domestic issues.' This reflects a broader tendency among some respondents to vote tactically, to oppose rather than support a party, or vote differentially in different types of election. For others, their vote was motivated less by policy concerns than by the religious identities of their local candidates or the party leaders. One respondent commented that the 'local Conservative candidate is a Christian therefore I will probably vote for him although I am really Labour in my thinking'. When asked about the reasons why they would vote for a particular candidate, only 28.9% of respondents to our 2014 *Faith in politics?* survey said their being a Christian was 'not important'. However, when asked which factor was 'most important of all', a much smaller proportion opted for this answer, with far more affirming the importance that the candidate be 'honourable and not corrupt'.

This relates to the most overwhelmingly evident perspective arising from this data: one of disillusionment with all of the major parties. When asked whether, compared to five years ago, they were more or less trusting of the government (or about the same), 59.4% said 'less', and 49.7% were less likely to believe what a politician says. Against this negative impression of compromise and broken promises, UKIP has acquired an image associated with conviction and principle that is clearly attractive to a small but significant number.

Nationalism and the devolved Parliaments

The nationalist cause associated with UKIP is articulated in terms of Great Britain – 'For a Britain Independent, Free and Fair', as the party website states. Not all are so keen on a united kingdom, however, and the subdivision of the UK into constituent countries, each with their own history, has engendered movements of a nationalist kind that are framed by a much more provincial set of boundaries, often defined over and against a dominant England and Westminster-based central government. Such nationalist causes have a much longer history than UKIP, and some have a more explicit relationship to Christian identities, calling upon Christian symbolism in affirming their cause and/or with popular support that coalesces along both religious and political lines. This is certainly the case in Northern Ireland, in which a long history of political turmoil and conflict has seen nationalist movements – calling for a united Ireland – associated with Roman Catholics, while unionist movements – maintaining the importance of unity with the rest of Britain – have often found expression among the Protestant communities.

Among those evangelicals who completed our baseline survey in 2010, 764 individuals were from Northern Ireland. Like other respondents, they were asked about their political party preference, although given the complex multi-party system in Ulster, the emerging picture is understandably different. The results are given in table 4.1, alongside the results of the popular vote in Northern Ireland in that same year's general election.

There are few surprises here, with the two parties most closely associated with the nationalist cause and Roman Catholic communities – Sinn Fein and the SDLP – receiving far less support among evangelicals than among the general population. Correspondingly, the unionist parties – the DUP and the Ulster Conservatives – received much more support, although not enough to make up the difference. These results reflect the close alignment between both 'evangelicalism' as an identity marker and the Protestant denominations, and between the Protestant denominations and the unionist cause in Northern Ireland. However, Ulster evangelicals demonstrate more than three times as much support than the population of the province as a whole for the Alliance party (20.8% compared to 6.3% of the NI vote). The Alliance Party was established in 1970 as a moderate unionist party,

Table 4.1 Party preferences of evangelicals living in Northern Ireland

	Voter support among Northern Ireland population	Stating as party of preference in baseline survey	Difference
Democratic Unionist Party	25.0%	37.2%	12.2
Sinn Fein	25.5%	0.5%	-25.0
Social Democratic & Labour Party	16.5%	6.8%	-9.7
Alliance Party	6.3%	20.8%	14.5
Ulster Conservatives and Unionists – New Force	15.2%	24.7%	9.5
Traditional Unionist Voice	3.9%	1.9%	-2.0
Green Party	0.5%	0.8%	0.3
Others	7.1%	7.1%	0

although in recent decades it has developed a neutral position on the issue of union with the UK, preferring to stand for a non-sectarian agenda in order to promote cooperation rather than division. Disproportionately high levels of support for the Alliance Party among evangelicals could suggest a strong endorsement of a post-sectarian, consensual agenda that is, for many, supplanting traditional party alignments.

The provincial boundaries of governance have also been subject to challenge and reconfiguration in other parts of the UK. Devolution was a New Labour project which saw significant powers devolved to national elected bodies in Scotland, Wales and Northern Ireland. The Scottish case was always the most significant, and after the Scottish National Party secured a majority in the Scottish Parliament in 2011, a campaign for Scottish independence was soon underway. The referendum on Scottish independence in September 2014 raised the prospect of the most radical redrawing of the UK's borders in 300 years, and campaigns from both sides of the debate revealed strong feelings and a divided Scotland (the 'no', pro-unionist camp prevailing with a relatively slim majority of 55.3% among a very high turnout of 84.6% of the electorate).

While perspectives differ within Scotland, the independence debate has triggered some renewed engagement in the political process, with the SNP standing out as an exception to widespread political disillusionment in attracting large numbers of new members in recent years (McGuinness, 2012). The debate has also generated reflection across the UK about its national identity, further resonating with discussions about our relationship to the rest of Europe. A question about Scottish independence was included in our *Are we good neighbours?* survey, and the overwhelming majority of evangelical respondents appeared firmly unionist in their position. In fact, 73.7% said they would be unhappy or very unhappy if Scotland became independent from the UK. Among those resident in Scotland, even more (75%) shared this position, so our evangelicals appear especially pro-unionist. The 'What Scotland Thinks' website, which tracks opinion polls on the independence issue, has opposition to independence among English and Welsh citizens at 63%, suggesting that our non-Scottish evangelicals are markedly more unionist than the nation as a whole. Whether this pattern has anything to do with their evangelicalism is unclear, although strongly embedded associations between Protestantism and British national identity are likely to be a factor for some.

Long-standing sectarian tendencies within certain parts of Northern Ireland and Scotland have highlighted how Protestantism can be co-opted into political movements of a nationalist character. The symbolic connection between Christian identity and British identity has also been exploited by UKIP as they seek to consolidate their grassroots appeal, with leader Nigel Farage calling for 'a much more muscular defence of our Judaeo-Christian heritage'. As Christians of various backgrounds emerge in concert with or passionately opposed to Farage's party, it will be interesting to observe whether such alignments feature more prominently in public debate in the 2015 general election campaign.

Evangelical values and political alignments

In the current climate, any debate about politics involves reflection on the widespread cynicism that apparently leaves many members of the electorate disillusioned with the political process. According to the British Election Study of 2010, 42.7% of the general population either agreed or agreed strongly with the statement, 'The main political parties in Britain don't offer voters real choices in elections because their policies are pretty much all the same'. A similar question in our 2014 *Faith in politics?* survey found 36.2% of evangelicals answering in the same way. Assuming the 2010 figures have not changed dramatically during the last four years, it would seem that our evangelical respondents are in keeping with country-wide levels of cynicism about the main political parties. Having said that, in the same survey, 79.8% said they were certain they would vote in the 2015 general election. The age profile of our respondents may mean that it includes a large number of individuals for whom political change is primarily achieved via the ballet box.

Evangelical Christians are commonly assumed to be preoccupied with issues of personal – and especially sexual – morality. There is some truth in this, and the importance of the same-sex marriage issue in shaping political orientations is a revealing illustration. However, the media appetite for personal controversy, together with the highly vocal campaigns concerning homosexuality and abortion among the US Christian Right, often colour popular opinion in a way that overshadows important complexities. A reorientation around a much broader range of political issues is especially evident within British evangelicalism. Moreover, the destabilisation of traditional party political alignments (see above) means that – as with the nation as a whole – we often learn a lot more about evangelicals' political values by examining their professed attitudes towards specific issues rather than by looking at how they cast their votes.

Broadly speaking, evangelicals appear to be fairly conservative on issues of theology and sexual ethics, while fairly left-leaning in their politics. More specifically, their political values appear strongly in favour of high taxes for the rich and lower taxes for the poor, and of government intervention to ensure fair working conditions for all and the eradication of injustice, including on the international stage. They are also strongly focused on issues of poverty and social inequality:

31.5% in 2014 state this as the 'single most important issue facing the UK today' (by far the most popular response, and compared to only 0.7% of the general population according to 2010 data collected as part of the British Election Study). Moreover, such patterns do not appear to be significantly different across age groups, although there are some exceptions. The under-35s express more uncertainty or more liberal inclinations with respect to assisted suicide and the blessing of civil partnerships in church, and yet are slightly more conservative with regard to abortion and women's roles in the church. More predictably, perhaps, younger respondents are less sympathetic than their older peers to the notion that the UK is a Christian country and that this should be reflected in its laws. There is also more wariness about immigration among older generations, for whom the jobs of British workers are more of a priority. Aside from these differences, comparable proportions oppose homosexual practice and sex outside marriage, support biblical inerrancy and tithing, and believe that it is a Christian's duty to volunteer in activities that serve the local community. In sum, there is some difference in values that can be associated with generational factors, but these differences are not dramatic, are outweighed by similarities, and do not follow an obvious pattern.

There is evidence that on a range of theological and moral issues, evangelical orientations are associated with their party political alignment. In 2010, we asked survey respondents how they had voted in that year's general election. Taking those who voted for the four main parties, it is possible to compare responses to questions and plot them on a broadly conceived conservative–liberal spectrum (see chart 4.1).

As can be seen, on issues of biblical inerrancy, assisted suicide, sex outside marriage and abortion, proportions affirming a conservative position are highest among UKIP voters and lowest among Lib-Dem voters, with the Conservative and Labour voters in between. Conversely, support for the notion that it is a Christian's duty to care for the environment follows the opposite pattern, with Lib-Dem voters most supportive and UKIP voters least. It is important to note that such a straightforward linear pattern is not in evidence on all issues, but nor is any alternative pattern consistently in evidence either. It would seem that party alignment among evangelicals can be

Chart 4.1 Evangelicals affirming they 'agree a lot' with various statements, according to 2010 baseline survey (P=<.001)

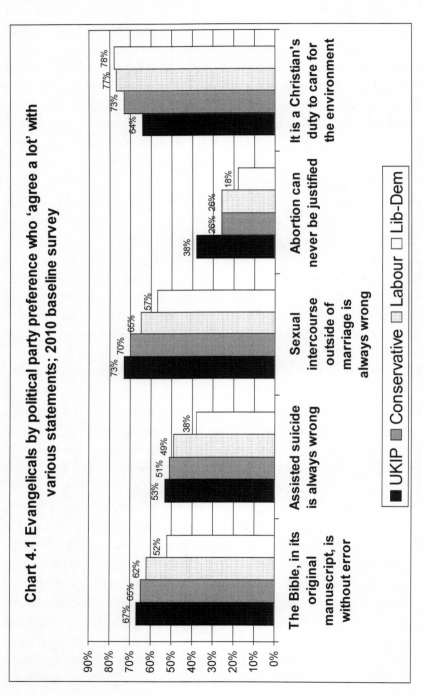

Chart 4.1 Evangelicals by political party preference who 'agree a lot' with various statements; 2010 baseline survey

■ UKIP ■ Conservative ▨ Labour □ Lib-Dem

associated with professed theological and moral values, and that these values can be placed along a conservative–liberal spectrum.

What this data also suggests is that, while disillusionment with the main political parties is widespread, the clusters of ideas and priorities associated with each of them remains, to some extent, intact. Further analysis will need to explore whether especially conservative Christians tend to gravitate towards UKIP or the Conservatives, or whether existing UKIP/Conservative supporters gravitate towards evangelical churches.

Conclusion

UK evangelicals are best known for their theological or moral convictions rather than their political persuasions, which remain less visible to the public eye. Unlike the situation in the United States, the evangelical vote has not become a major factor in national elections, partly on account of the smaller proportion of evangelicals in the UK, and partly because of our political history. The Christian parties of the European continent did not emerge here as there were already close affinities between the Roman Catholics and Labour, the non-conformists and the Liberals, and the Tories and the established Church of England. This historical splitting of the Christian vote also diluted its capacity as a force of political influence, which was diminished further by ever-increasing religious nominalism within all three factions.

Within this context, politically engaged evangelicalism has emerged from the margins with no clear affinity with any single political party. This is reflected in the data discussed above, illustrating that, in terms of party political support, evangelicals are not significantly dissimilar from the UK population at large. However, political orientations among evangelicals do coalesce around certain tendencies and issues, suggesting their evangelical identities are significant to their political perspectives, albeit in complex and subtle ways.

The Christian think tank Theos published a report in 2013 entitled 'Is There a "Religious Right" Emerging in Britain?' The report concludes in the negative, referring to the tendency of UK evangelicals – in contrast with those in the US – to be economically left-of-centre, interested in an overlapping but also quite different set of moral issues, and lacking any enduring alignment with a single political party whose interests are seen to echo their own. Our own data confirms this picture, suggesting an evangelical population which, while fairly conservative on theological issues and on issues of sexual morality, nevertheless also tends to affirm perspectives on global justice, financial propriety, poverty and inequality that are most often associated with the progressive left. This does not translate into majority support for Labour or the Liberal Democrats, however, and evangelicals appear to be just as disillusioned with the main political parties as the rest of the population, some having diverted their support to Christian parties or UKIP in the years following the 2010 election.

This disillusionment is, for some, reinforced by cross-party support for the same-sex marriage Act in 2013, suggesting that issues of personal morality can be a shaping influence over the Christian vote. Here is where the UK and US evangelical movements appear most alike, while also radically different. According to sociologists Robert Putnam and David Campbell, the US coalition of the religious that has lent dependable support to the Republican Party in recent decades depends in part on sex and family issues remaining at stake in an election (Putnam and Campbell, 2010: 414). UK elections are typically not won or lost on issues such as abortion or sexual morality; instead, voters are most interested in the economy and its impact on their own welfare. The Conservative Party have attempted to use the rhetoric of family values to woo the electorate, but with mixed success, and a general liberal consensus across the main three parties – especially on free market economics and respect for individual freedoms – has alienated those who hold a more traditional perspective on issues of family, gender and sexuality. The rise of UKIP can be seen, in part, as a consequence of this, and its emergence as a symbol of British traditionalism has influenced a small but not insignificant proportion of evangelical voters. The future will reveal whether this indicates a more general shift towards a more 'values-based' politics, and what role evangelical Christians will have as the political landscape continues to change.

References

Heath, Anthony & Khan, Omar (2012). 'Ethnic Minority British Election Study – Key Findings'. Available at http://www.runnymedetrust.org/uploads/EMBESbriefingFINALx.pdf (accessed 12th August 2014).

Hunt, Stephen & Lightly, Nicola (2001). 'The British black Pentecostal "revival": identity and belief in the "new" Nigerian churches'. *Ethnic and Racial Studies* Vol 24, Issue 1, pp.104–124. Available at http://www.tandfonline.com/toc/rers20/24/1#.VJf_iUoKA (accessed 24th December 2014).

Ipsos MORI. 'How Britain Voted in 2010'. Available at http://www.ipsos-mori.com/researchpublications/researcharchive/2613/How-Britain-Voted-in (accessed 1st August 2014).

McGuinness, Feargal (2012). 'Membership of Political Parties', House of Commons Library, p.5.

Putnam, Robert & Campbell, David (2010). *American Grace: How Religion Divides and Unites Us*. New York: Simon & Schuster.

What Scotland Thinks, 'Do you support or oppose Scottish independence from the UK? (English/ Welsh view)'. Available at http://whatscotlandthinks.org/questions/do-you-support-or-oppose-scottish-independence-from-the-uk-english-welsh-view-1#lin (accessed 17th December 2014).

Theos. 'Is There a "Religious Right" Emerging in Britain?' (2013). Available at http://www.theosthinktank.co.uk/files/files/Reports/IS%20THERE%20A%20RELIGIOUS%20RIGHT%20%28NEW%29.pdf (accessed 24th December 2014).

Response to chapter 4

Stephen Timms MP

Matthew has identified a high level of interest in politics among evangelicals. But many evangelicals feel they don't have much impact on Britain's politics. I believe they are under-estimating their influence.

The negative view has been reinforced by David Cameron's same-sex marriage legislation. Evangelicals did not appear to have much impact on the debate. Many used to trust the Conservative Party to safeguard traditional moral values. They feel let down.

But elsewhere I believe evangelicals have wielded profound influence on British politics. Among the most striking survey findings are the strong support for tackling injustice, including on the international stage, and that 33.6% of evangelicals see poverty and social inequality as 'the single most important issue facing the UK', compared to 0.7% of the general population. It has come as a surprise to many that – given escalating food poverty in Britain since 2010 – church-based foodbanks have provided the most effective response. It has turned out that churches, uniquely, have had both the motivation and the resources to help.

On the international stage, Jubilee 2000 and, in 2005, Make Poverty History were supported mainly by churches. Organisers of both estimated that 80% of those who sent postcards to MPs and attended demonstrations were church members, and many will have been evangelicals. The last Labour government, under their influence, promised an international aid budget of at least 0.7% of GDP.

The incoming Conservative-led government, focused on deficit reduction, might have been expected to abandon this commitment. New ministers had no hesitation in scrapping costly programmes they had previously said they would keep, and raising taxes they said they would not raise. But they did not abandon the 0.7% target, despite pressure from Conservative backbenchers to do so. They have now delivered the target.

The reason for the consensus on the 0.7% target, and for such a costly commitment surviving the change of government, is in my view clear: it is because churches lobbied so enthusiastically for it. Church support lifted it above party squabbling. And much of that energy in the churches came from evangelicals.

We see something similar now in the campaign against human trafficking, and the debate around the Modern Slavery Bill. Evangelicals need to realise that – contrary to what is often said – they can have a very substantial impact on UK politics.

Those taking part in politics from a starting point of Christian faith bring with them values which can make politics work, and of which we need more. Starting with the campaign against slavery – the first great popular democratic campaign in history – evangelicals made an enormous contribution to parliamentary democracy. If they step forward now to work with others in the hard graft of political decision making, including joining a political party, evangelicals can play a major part in transforming politics and making it deserving of trust once again.

Rt Hon Stephen Timms has been MP for East Ham since 1994. He is shadow employment minister and Chair of Christians on the Left.

Chapter 5: Evangelicals and gender

Sylvia Collins-Mayo

The social world has changed enormously over the last 50 years, and this has impacted on how we understand men and women and their relationship to one another. Traditional notions of masculinity and femininity have been challenged, and gender is recognised as an important aspect of identity and difference, social justice and equality. While none of the 11 *21st Century Evangelicals* surveys specifically focused on gender as a topic per se, the results from across the studies provide some interesting and important findings concerning the differences and similarities between men and women on a host of issues. The purpose of this chapter is to elaborate these findings to obtain a clearer sense of how evangelicalism is 'gendered'.

It has already been noted that the survey participants are not necessarily representative of all evangelicals in the UK. In terms of gender, men are slightly over-represented and women under-represented to what we might expect, and the imbalance is particularly strong among the older age groups. The 2011 Census figures for England indicate that around 46% of Christians are men. The 2005 English Church Census suggests that, depending on denomination and 'churchmanship', church congregations are between 40% and 48% male (Brierley, 2006). Our surveys were therefore unusual in that men made up 50% to 55% of the participants.

Notwithstanding these demographics, the data can still be used to explore how male and female participants are different or similar to each other in their attitudes and behaviours. This at least raises our awareness of gender in evangelical contexts, which in turn may prompt discussion, further exploration and, where necessary, a response. The focus of this chapter is on participants who answered 'Yes' to the question, 'Do you consider yourself to be an evangelical Christian?' – which is around 90% of the sample.

Gender

Social scientists make a distinction between 'sex' and 'gender'. 'Sex' refers to the biological characteristics that make us male or female and tends to be presented as a stable binary category, even though there are some individuals whose physical attributes do not conform to a neat male/female divide. 'Gender', on the other hand, is less about biology (male and female) and more about ideology and social meanings – what it means to be a man or woman (masculinity and femininity). As such, gender is a fluid and diverse concept. Sex may form the raw material of gender, but how gender is experienced and lived out is a result of socially defined norms, roles, values and expectations that express particular understandings of maleness and femaleness at any given time in particular contexts. These understandings order and structure our relationships with one another and convey notions of identity and power. In British society (as in most societies) the balance of power has been, and continues to be, in favour of men.

Although less significant in its general influence over social attitudes today, historically the male-led church, alongside other institutions, has played an important part in ensuring that men have freedoms, opportunities and responsibilities denied to women. Church teachings and practices over the centuries have helped to define and legitimise particular expressions of femininity and masculinity over others. Theologies, language, symbols and rituals that enact and explain the differences between men and women as part of God's created order have had a powerful hold over the collective psyche and people's sense of what they should and should not do, both inside and outside of church.

However, because gender meanings are socially determined, they are also open to challenge and change. In this respect, the gendered order is not simply 'given' and imposed on people; it is also continually worked at, negotiated and reproduced or modified in everyday interactions. Men and women collectively and individually have a degree of agency in the maintenance or subversion of traditional gender norms. Over the last century, and particularly since the 1960s, we have seen changes in wider society, led by feminists and the women's movement, that the church has sometimes struggled to keep up with. The data from the surveys helps us to see where evangelicals as individuals maintain and challenge gender norms.

Gender is not, of course, the only variable to structure the social world and inform our identities. Class, ethnicity, sexuality and age, among other factors, also determine how we experience and live out our lives, and therefore how gender is expressed. This makes for greater variation than is indicated simply by talk of differences between men and women. There are often more differences among women and among men than there are between women and men. For example, a young woman of colour living and working in a deprived inner-city area may have more in common with her young male neighbour than with a white middle-aged woman living in an affluent suburb. These complications are beyond the analysis of this chapter, but it is worth bearing in mind that the participants in the surveys tend to be older, white and middle class. This will influence the gender differences we find.

Marriage and family life

While all institutions uphold the gender order of the society in which they are based, it is the family that provides the primary socialisation of individuals into gender roles. Even before they are born, babies are subject to speculation about their sex. Once they enter the world, almost everything around them takes on a gendered dimension – colours, clothes, toys, activities, language, relationships with carers and so on: they all carry gender meanings and assumptions. Even the most determined parents find it difficult to keep their children in a gender-neutral environment; conscious efforts to do so in the home are easily outweighed by influences from wider culture. Consequently, children learn many of the same gender norms their parents learnt when they were growing up: little girls learn that part of being a woman is to marry, raise children and look after a home and a husband. This remains the case even when they learn that another part of womanhood is to enter the labour market and have a career. Boys learn that their role is to make a mark in the world, to lead, to be successful and to gain other people's respect, to support their family financially if they marry but not necessarily to get involved with domestic or emotional concerns.

Of course, family forms are changing, and as men and women take on different roles within and outside the home, so attitudes to gender roles slowly change too. Yet the 'traditional' idea of a family, where the woman's primary responsibilities are as mother and homemaker and the man's are as breadwinner and head, remains a strong motif with an attitudinal legacy. Within the church, as elsewhere, normative family ideals have been challenged by divorce and remarriage, single parenthood, women's paid employment and changing attitudes to sexuality, but church teaching and discourse still tends to hold heterosexual marriage and loving family relationships as the bedrock of emotional well-being, the mainstay of material support and the best environment for childcare and nurture. So what do evangelicals think?

Among the (1,219) participants in the *How's the family?* survey, around three-quarters are or have been married, but the men are more likely to be (or have been) married than the women (84% compared to 73%). There may be a number of reasons for this gender difference. One is that it is common for churches to advocate that Christians marry within the faith (two-thirds of our participants think this is their current church's view) but, put simply, there are not enough men to go around. From an institutional perspective there are good reasons for promoting intra-faith marriages, not least of which is that couples where both partners are churchgoers are twice as likely to raise churchgoing children than couples where only one partner goes to church (Voas and Crockett, 2005). Nevertheless, the injunction to marry within the faith means that more women than men are denied the chance of matrimony and the family life that normally follows. Yet for the most part it seems that evangelical men and women abide by the 'rules': of our participants who were committed Christians at the time of their wedding, nearly all the men (97%) and most of the women (87%) married a committed Christian.

Following on from this, a quarter of our female participants are single. Aune's (2002) study of single women in the church highlights some of the concerns they have in relation to their single status, which include feelings of loneliness, worries about dating and sex, concerns about not having children and a sense of exclusion from aspects of church life. Attitudes towards singleness among our participants (both married and single) show similarities between men and women. Around three-quarters think that marrieds and singles are well integrated into the life of their church and that their church recognises and affirms the gifts and contribution of single people in 'most aspects of its ministry and leadership'. Roughly a quarter (23%), however, think that their church values married couples and families more than single people, which, if true, means that women are particularly vulnerable to being ignored or overlooked.

Just over half (58%) of men and women said that many single Christians have a difficult life, but men (73%) are significantly more likely than women (59%) to say that Christian singles face lots of sexual frustrations and temptations. Moreover, only 21% of participants think that their church provides good teaching on issues around singleness and support of single people.

Looking on the positive side, 82% of men and 74% of women regard singleness as providing an opportunity for a lifestyle dedicated to God and mission. But this opportunity is gendered since the single life for women does not necessarily lead to the same freedoms that it does for men. Furthermore, male roles in church are not normally dependent on having a spouse, whereas some of the evangelical women in Aune's (2002) study commented on being excluded from certain roles because of their single status. This occurred in churches where male 'covering' was seen as important for women in positions of authority.

Among our participants, traditional ideas of a woman as carer and a man as head of the family are still held by many, albeit that they are gradually changing as younger people are less traditional in their thinking than older people. Just over half of men (58%) and women (51%) agree that a 'Christian husband should exercise headship over the wife', and just under half of men (45%) and women (49%) agree that a 'woman's main role in a family is to care for and nurture the children' (these gender differences are not statistically significant). Interestingly, when taking the age of participants into consideration, it is younger *men* rather than women who show the greatest shift in attitude. Sixty per cent of men in their fifties or older agree with male headship and 51% that the woman's main role in the family is to care for and nurture children, whereas only 54% of men under 50 agree with male headship and only 35% that the woman's main role is to care and nurture. By contrast, 50% of women over 50 and 51% of women under 50 agree with male headship. Fifty-six per cent of older women, compared to 44% of younger women, agree that the woman's main role in the family is childcare.

In accepting and living out these views, gender roles are reproduced. In this respect, two-thirds of the participants who are or who have been parents suggested that when their children were young, it generally was the woman 'who did/does almost all the housework' and 'almost all the childcare', although only 6% said that it 'is/was father who makes/made all the important decisions'. We need to note here that participants are going on their recollections in answering these questions, as many would have been bringing up their children several decades ago. All the participants thought that 'fathers should be fully involved in caring for and raising their children', although just what constitutes 'fully involved' is open to interpretation.

Overall, the survey shows that traditional gender roles in the family remain a part of the evangelical psyche. However, things are gradually changing. Women, for example, are more open to the validity of non-traditional families, even if they might want to have a traditional family life themselves. Nearly half of the women (45%) compared to just a third of men (30%) agree that there 'are many different types of family today and we should accept all of them as equal'. Similarly, women (64%) are *less likely* than men (79%) to agree that Christians should vigorously oppose 'gay marriage'.

Whatever gender roles might be played out in their own families, it is encouraging to find that the majority of married participants are happy with their marriages. Men (72%) were slightly more inclined to say they are 'very happy' than women (65%), but the differences are not statistically significant. A further 24% of married women and 19% of married men said they are 'fairly happy'. Yet despite a generally positive picture, it is troubling that just over a quarter of participants who describe themselves as currently married, cohabiting or having been married in the past, particularly women (32%), have on at least one occasion received emotional or verbal abuse within their marriage – 5% said they have experienced it 'frequently'. Nine percent have been subject to physical violence or abuse at least once in their marriage – again women (14%) more than men (5%).

Domestic abuse is a significant problem in society, but much goes unreported. Data from the Crime Survey for England and Wales in

2011–2012 suggests that around 31% of women and 18% of men in the general population have experienced some sort of domestic abuse since the age of 16 (Dar, 2013). It is quite possible that Christians are less likely to report domestic violence than non-religious people since it contradicts the Christian call to love one another and therefore undermines Christian identity. Lest we think the problem in church lies primarily with Christians married to non-Christian partners, among those who were committed Christians when they got married and who married committed Christians, 21% have received emotional or verbal abuse, and 4% have received physical violence or abuse from their partner 'frequently' or 'on more than one occasion'. Again, women are more likely to be victims than men.

Looking at things the other way around, a quarter of men and women admit to having *given* emotional or verbal abuse in their marriage at least once, and 6% said they have given physical abuse at least once (there is no difference between men and women on these variables). Nine per cent of the men and 8% of the women admit to having been unfaithful to their partner at least once. (Five per cent of men and 12% of women know their partner has been unfaithful to them at least once.)

None of this makes happy reading. Just over a quarter of the men and women who have found themselves in difficulty within their marriage have sought some sort of counselling or other professional help. Perhaps because women are more likely to be at the sharp end of relationship difficulties, or because they are expected to be relationally literate, women (33%) are more likely than men (25%) to have sought such help for their marriage, although both men and women have read books, attended marriage enrichment seminars or talked to friends about their marriage in order to strengthen and improve it.

Individuals who commented on their counselling report a mixed set of experiences in terms of how helpful it was. Worryingly, several people indicated that theological stances had sometimes taken precedence over pastoral need when help was sought from their church: 'The church disowned me because I left my husband after years of sexual abuse,' wrote one woman; another commented that her 'pastor's attitude was that I was not submissive enough'.

Work life

Outside of the family, paid work is another aspect of life that is highly gendered in British society for, despite all the advances that have been made in terms of equal opportunities, it is still the case that social status and material rewards are more likely to go to men than women. Of course, many Christians may want to eschew these 'worldly' things and regard 'status' in the eyes of God and heavenly rewards as more important, at least in relation to their own employment. Nevertheless, issues of gender inequality and injustice should still concern Christians. The gendered nature of work shows itself up in the types of jobs men and women do, the grade levels they achieve in organisations, the amount of pay they receive and their vulnerability to harassment.

Early socialisation and gender stereotypes as to what counts as men's and women's work play an important part in shaping the careers in which people end up. For older people in the workforce, education and training opportunities were more gendered than they are today. Consequently girls commonly ended up in administration, caring and other service jobs, for example, while boys went into construction, engineering, transport and so on. Even today, however, where boys and girls have equal access to school curricula, the aspirations and choices of young people remain gendered. For example, the Women's Engineering Society cites, 'Only 7% of the engineering workforce in the UK is female,' and 'Nearly half (46%) of all co-ed secondary state schools sent no girls on to do physics at A level in 2011.' This is despite the fact that girls tend to do better than boys in science subjects at GCSE level.

The segregation of the workforce reinforces the pay gap between men and women since female-dominated occupations tend to attract lower wages than male-dominated occupations. This inequality is not entirely explained by skill differences between male and female jobs, but rather reflects a systematic social undervaluation of women's work (Perales, 2011).

Once in an occupation, women's access to promotion is often hampered by employers (deliberately or unconsciously) continuing to overlook them. Despite the illegality of this practice, it is time consuming as well as emotionally and practically difficult for individual women to challenge sex discrimination cases. It can also be prohibitively expensive if legal representation is needed to sort out disputes. Career breaks in order to have children or care for relatives also slows women's advancement in relation to men, as does inflexible working practices which make it hard for women to do full-time paid work as well as tend to the lion's share of caring responsibilities that is expected of them at home.

The UK Household Longitudinal Study (Kan, 2012) indicates that married women of working age do three-quarters of the housework in their homes, and even though the amount of housework goes down and becomes more evenly distributed between men and women as women contribute to the family income, they still do more housework than men. Furthermore, when women earn more than 65% of the family income, the amount of time women spend on housework actually *increases* rather than decreases. Perhaps women are trying to compensate for challenging gender norms 'too much'. On the other hand, 'Men who earn more than their wives do little housework' (Kan, 2012:8). The same can be said for childcare and other family care work – the bulk of it is done by women (Scott and Clery, 2013:126). One might reasonably conclude that where traditional gender roles remain in the home and non-traditional roles develop in the workplace, married men end up rather better off than their working wives!

In the results of our (1,382) participants in the *Working faithfully?* survey, the above gender distinctions are apparent. As women's participation in the labour market has increased considerably since the 1960s, so nearly all (99%) of the participants have at some time in their life been in paid employment. At the time of completing the survey, just under two-thirds of men (63%) and women (59%) were in paid work, either as an employee or self-employed. Less than 1% of men and 3% of women describe themselves as a 'full-time homemaker or carer'. Of those in work, most people are in the education, health, service, public or voluntary sectors (68% of women and 45% of men). These have traditionally been female-dominated occupations but they also appeal to individuals wanting to make a positive impact on the social world, which fits with the Christian ethos of helping others and may therefore be attractive to Christian men as well as women.

Only 6% of women, compared to 20% of men, are in traditionally male-dominated occupations such as manufacturing, construction, transport, mining, farming and finance. Nineteen per cent of women and 24% of men work for church or Christian organisations, and 7% of women and 11% of men work in 'other' employment sectors. More men (29%) than women (16%) occupy senior management positions. Consequently, nearly three-quarters of men (72%) compared to around two-thirds (64%) of women said they feel involved in decisions that affect their work. Men tend to work longer hours than women, which reflects women's preference for part-time work as they juggle home responsibilities with paid employment. These factors together lead to women having a lower level of take-home pay than men: 56% of working women compared to 31% of working men take home £1,500 or less per month; 35% of women compared to 50% of men take home between £1,501 and £3,000; 15% of men and 3% of women take home £3,000 or more each month. Only 51% of women compared to 59% of men said that they feel adequately paid. With more influence and money, it is clear that men retain the power to shape their own life experiences and to shape the lives of women too.

Although men and women tend to do different types of work and are paid differently, on a number of measures of job satisfaction there is little difference in participants' experiences. Most of those in paid employment, for example, feel valued for their work, are interested in it and are treated with respect by colleagues. Sixty per cent think they achieve a good work–life balance, although a quarter do not think they have an acceptable workload and 38% said they often feel stressed because of work. Women (74%) are significantly more inclined than men (67%) to say they have a strong sense of calling to their work.

When it comes to thinking about what is desirable in a job, women have more criteria than men as to what counts as 'very important': they tend to prioritise relational factors and the convenience of the job as it fits with the rest of their life, whereas men rate material factors such as pay, career prospects, pension provision and benefits as 'very important'. These in some ways fit with stereotypical notions of women as relational and men as rational and materialistic. However, the two factors which stand out for men and (especially) women as to what would make a job desirable are: (1) 'Knowing God has answered your prayers for guidance and opened doors to get you the job,' and (2) 'Good attitudes and practices of management.' These are more gender-neutral factors, although just what counts as 'good management' may differ in the eyes of men and women. The *Time for discipleship?* survey indicates that women are more likely than men to say they see prayers being answered (89% of women compared to 78% of men) and to see God at work in their life on a daily basis (79% of women compared to 74% of men).

The *Working faithfully?* survey asked panel members a few questions on gender issues in the workplace based on their own experience or that of colleagues, family and friends. The responses suggest that gender discrimination has quite a low salience for most of the participants, and few identify themselves as having been subject to discrimination themselves. Less than two-thirds of women and less than half of men agree that, 'Women often encounter obstacles that prevent their progression to the top level of their career structure,' and that, 'Many very capable women are trapped in low-pay, low-status and insecure jobs.'

Only 41% of women and 37% of men think sexual harassment remains a significant problem in the workplace. Both men and women are inclined to think that discrimination on the grounds of (old) age or disability is more prevalent than discrimination against women. Thirteen per cent of women and 10% of men said they have been subject to discrimination at work. When asked to give details, ageism and prejudice against Christianity were cited by many; sexism was described by far fewer people, though reference to it was by no means absent. One woman wrote, 'Am very overqualified for my job yet cannot get promoted. Instead I see far less able men promoted. Women are mainly confined to the lower grade jobs.' Another simply said, 'Well, if I want to be a bishop…!?!' It was also noted that sexism can go both ways. One man described his experiences as follows:

> I was in a mainly female workforce, sometimes collectively addressed 'girls'. In team meetings when patients were discussed there was sometimes anti-men 'humour'. ('Why is Mr Smith still in bed? Because he's a man.')

Another man expressed a hint of resentfulness towards policy practices that seek to redress the gender imbalance for promotion:

I've seen awards and promotions go to women who seem less deserving than other candidates. There is an ethos of 'positive discrimination' creeping into our workplaces.

Discipleship

The above findings suggest that 'traditional' gender norms continue to influence evangelicals' family and work life, even if attitudes and practices are slowly changing in line with gender norms in wider society. Chapter 2 has shown in detail how traditional gender roles are manifest in church life where male leadership remains dominant and women tend to take on nurturing roles such as participating in children's and youth work or providing refreshments.

Church life is the public face of Christian commitment. This last section considers the more private aspects of religious expression in terms of how men and women differ in their discipleship.

The *Time for discipleship?* survey asked (1,529) participants to indicate which of Jesus' followers in the New Testament they most closely identify with. This tells us something about how people perceive their own character and circumstances. Women generally identify with women and men with men. Given that women still retain most of the domestic and caring responsibilities at home but are also likely to be in some sort of paid work as well, it is little wonder that more of the women (58%) identified with 'Martha – busy with the tasks of everyday life' than with 'Mary (sister of Martha) who sat at the feet of Jesus and listened' (25%). Men have a greater selection of characters to choose from, but the most common choices are those that emphasise leadership rather than relationship – that is, stereotypical male characteristics: 37% of men identify with 'Simon Peter – the bold leader who always spoke up but often let Jesus down,' and 35% with 'Paul – the evangelist, thinker and theologian.' This compares to just 20% of men identifying with 'John – the close friend.'

In terms of who has inspired participants on their faith journeys, the strength of the male voice becomes apparent in that the top ten Christian authors, speakers or leaders identified were all men; as indeed were most historical figures. Mother Teresa, Jackie Pullinger and Corrie Ten Boom, however, did receive some mention. Closer to home, around a quarter of the participants said their mother was an inspiration; fathers slightly less so, but were more influential for men (24%) than women (19%). Men (33%) were significantly more likely to identify their wives as an inspiration, compared to women (20%) identifying their husbands.

Evangelical spirituality which places an emphasis on a personal relationship with Christ points to the importance of a daily 'quiet time' for prayer and Bible reading in which the relationship can be fostered. The significance of a quiet time is recognised by the participants in the *Time for discipleship?* survey as 87% agree with the statement, 'Every Christian needs to spend time alone with God on a daily basis – without that their faith will suffer.' In practice, this is not always achievable: women in particular (46% compared to 38% of men) said that they find it difficult to pray on a regular, disciplined basis. Perhaps women's commitments are less easily structured than men's to develop a set routine, or perhaps they see taking time out of their other responsibilities as somewhat self-indulgent. That said, just under half of women (46%) and just over half of men (54%) said that they engage with the Bible at least once every day (a further 37% of men and 44% of women do so several times a week), usually for between 10 and 20 minutes at a time. In addition, around a third of men and women said that they have one or more substantial periods of prayer time every day, which results in 43% of men and women spending at least an hour in private prayer each week.

The things women say they find helpful in their devotional life differs from men in that women are more likely to make use of material artefacts, creative resources and their bodies. Thus women more than men find it helpful to have a special prayer place at home, to make use of particular body postures when praying, to listen or sing to music, to light a candle, to pray 'on the move' (e.g. when travelling) and to create a list of people to pray for. Half of women, compared to just over a quarter of men (29%), have kept a journal to help their discipleship; nearly a third of women (32%) have gone on retreats (26% of men have done so), and two-thirds have attended conventions (compared to 60% of men). It therefore seems that women are more inclined to try different ways of developing their discipleship than men.

Women also tend to draw on more relational support than men do. This is not surprising given that women are socialised to prioritise relationships in their lives. A third of women, for example, find having a spiritual director or being part of a small group such as a prayer triplet very helpful, compared to only 20% of men. The significance of relationships to women is also reflected in the meaning of prayer. Half of women compared to 40% of men said the most important purpose of prayer is to 'bring you into a closer relationship with God.'

Finally, to sin! It is often suggested that girls as future mothers and carers are raised under a stricter moral regime than boys. Boys tend to have greater independence at an earlier age than girls, and young men have more sexual licence than young women. The old adage, 'Boys will be boys,' goes some way to dismissing youthful transgressions for which girls would be taken to task. Girls are also put under a lot of social pressure to conform to particular standards of female body image and beauty as well as behaviour.

Looking at the differences between the temptations men and women say they face, it is possible to see the influence of these gendered expectations on participants' perceptions of guilt and failure. Women are more likely than men to say they are 'often guilty' of subjective failings such as being self-centred, of having judgemental attitudes and of having feelings of despair, worry or anxiety. In other words, they see themselves as falling short of the heavy demands of being emotionally present for others and also being accepted by others. The only temptation that men seem to significantly struggle with more than women is pornography. Of the 'seven deadly sins', women are more inclined than men to say that they commit the sins of gluttony, sloth, envy and pride, whereas for men the main sin is lust. There is no significant gender difference in terms of succumbing to wrath or greed.

Concluding thought

A phrase sometimes used in church circles is that men and women are 'different but equal'. The findings from the *21st Century Evangelicals* surveys somewhat challenge this maxim. In many respects our men and women are similar in their beliefs and attitudes. Even when they do differ, the disparities are not great. Similarities reflect the fact that our participants, though different in sex, have much in common otherwise. Not least, they all participate in the dominant culture of British society at large and the narrower subculture of evangelical Christianity. Norms, values and shared meanings are derived from these cultural spheres and mutually held, including those relating to gender. Of course, sometimes Christian norms and values clash with those of 'the world', and evangelicals have to work out how to respond, but our men and women are sharing the same cultural 'stuff' in doing so.

Where our men and women are different is in the opportunities and experiences that gender norms afford them – and in this, men and women are not equal. We have seen that traditional family ideas remain important for many evangelical men and women, yet women are more likely than men to suffer domestic abuse, and women who struggle to find a Christian partner have fewer freedoms than men who remain single. When evangelical women enter the labour market, which most of them do, like their non-evangelical 'sisters' they are likely to receive less pay and fewer promotion opportunities than their male colleagues. They are also likely to retain the bulk of household duties and care work at home. In church, women's leadership skills are often overlooked in favour of men's and, as such, it is the male voice that has the greater influence on the norms of church life and discipleship.

Things are changing, albeit slowly. One of the values of the *21st Century Evangelicals* surveys is that they highlight where evangelicals can take action for equality and justice – from educating church members about domestic violence, to working towards inclusive congregations that celebrate single as well as family life, to taking social action for gender equality in the wider world, to changing church practices so that women and men have a truly equal voice. Gender discrimination is not just a 'women's issue', and it requires both men and women to work together to bring about equality. We're not there yet!

References

Aune, K. (2002). *Single Women: Challenge to the Church?* London: Paternoster Press.

Brierley, P. (2006). *Pulling Out of the Nosedive: A contemporary picture of churchgoing,* London: Christian Research.

Dar, A. (2013). *Domestic Violence Statistics,* House of Commons Library Standard Note SN/SG/950.

Kan, M. Y. (2012). 'Revisiting the 'doing gender' hypothesis – housework hours of husbands and wives in the UK', in McFall, S.L (ed). *Understanding Society: Findings 2012,* Colchester: Institute for Social and Economic Research, University of Essex, pp.7-8.

Perales, F. (2011). 'Why does the work women do pay less than the work men do?', *Case Study – Research,* UK Data Service. Available at http://ukdataservice.ac.uk/use-data/data-in-use/case-study/?id=62 (accessed 20th August 2014).

Scott, J. & Clery, E. (2013). 'Gender roles: An incomplete revolution?' in Park, A., Bryson, C., Clery, E., Curtice, J. & Philips, M. (eds). *British Social Attitudes: The 30th Report,* London: NatCen Social Research, pp.115-139.

Voas, D. & Crockett, A. (2005). 'Religion in Britain: Neither believing nor belonging', *Sociology,* Vol. 39, No. 1, pp.11-28.

Women's Engineering Society (2014). 'Statistics on Women's Engineering'. Available at http://www.wes.org.uk/statistics (accessed 20th August 2014).

Response to chapter 5: Evangelicals and gender

Elaine Duncan

On one of my visits to the Bible Society in Peru, I was privileged to witness a training seminar on gender equality. This was being held in a rural church high up in the Andes and was the first in a series of seminars in which the church and the Bible Society are working in partnership to tackle the huge social problem of domestic violence. This part of Peru holds very traditional social values about the role of men and women: 75% of households experience domestic violence. I was so encouraged to see the church taking a lead in addressing this enormous and serious social problem, and doing so from a biblical basis.

The church in the UK has not been seen to take such a lead on these issues and, as Sylvia points out, we have generally been slow to catch up with changes in the culture in which we live. Our theological understanding and interpretations of Scripture have differed so much within the evangelical world that we have not been able to speak clearly and with one voice into areas that are of deep significance to at least half the population.

This is not the place for long theological argument, but even if we start with Genesis 1:26-27 we find that when God created human beings in His image, it involved two sexes. So I conclude that it is as male and female **together** that we reflect the image of God. This is the basis of our absolute equality. This chapter shows that we still have a way to go in seeing that expressed fully and deeply within our homes, our churches and our places of work. I hope, as Sylvia does, that the results shown in this survey will lead us to more discussion, greater exploration and active responses.

We live in a world where violence and abuse of women and children is far too commonplace, and violence against men is increasing too. It is good to see Christians take up the cause against human trafficking, gender-based violence and female genital mutilation. But I still wonder if we have been a little slow off the mark in these areas, rather than being those who give a lead to others in our wider society.

The view of and treatment of women in other faiths is also an issue we have to address. Political correctness can sometimes hold us back from speaking out against injustice, violence and deep inequality as we see it expressed in other faith traditions. We must find ways to challenge injustice and inequality. Of course, we can only do that with integrity if we are addressing the issues within our own communities of the church.

There is much in this chapter to stimulate discussion. My prayer is that we will be willing to engage in constructive discourse and be open to the leading and guiding of the Holy Spirit as we explore this area more fully. We are followers of the Lord Jesus who consistently conferred dignity and value on the women He encountered, in an even more patriarchal culture than we have in the UK today. May we have grace to follow in His footsteps, male and female together.

Elaine Duncan is the Chief Executive of the Scottish Bible Society.

Chapter 6: Evangelical families, children and youth

Keith J. White

There have been significant observable changes in the nature of marriage, households and families in British society within the last two generations. These have been accompanied by changes in attitudes towards and in the understanding of personal relationships and of childhood, parenting and youth. In this chapter we explore how far such observable changes, and also changes of attitude and understanding, are reflected in the lives, experience and thinking of evangelical Christians.

An example of observable change is the way in which marriage itself has been redefined by the passing of the Marriage (Same Sex Couples) Act 2013, which received Royal Assent on 17th July 2013, and the first marriage of a same-sex couple which took place on 29th March 2014. The surveys on which this chapter is based do not investigate this issue, but we know from some of our other surveys and from their campaigning that most evangelicals, with their tendency to a traditional reading of the Bible as a basis for norms and lifestyles, will be challenged by the change. That provision is made in the legislation for churches and other faith groups to continue with their accepted ceremonies and norms represents an acknowledgement that laws of state may be in tension with religious beliefs and traditions.

Quite apart from such tangible legal changes, there has been a remarkably clear trend towards the acceptability of cohabitation ('living together') outside of marriage. In the mid-1960s, just 5% of single women lived with a man before getting married. Thirty years later this was true of 70% (Haskey, 1995). It is no longer seen as a preparation to marriage, but rather as an alternative. Cohabitation has become an accepted norm, and descriptions of it have changed from 'living in sin' to 'partners living together'. And it is an accepted norm for the children of either member of that couple who live in the same household.

But when compared to marriage, cohabitation is a distinctly different form of relationship for each partner, for the children, and for society in that usually there is no formal agreement about the terms (and term) of the relationship. In practice, 96% of cohabitations end within ten years (Ermisch & Francesconi, 1998). One of the key factors when considering families or households is how this trend from publicly affirmed marriage to privately assumed cohabitation might affect children.

Although it is indisputable that children of married couples may suffer neglect and or abuse, it is widely accepted that children thrive in the context of stable and committed parental relationships. Such a context allows bonds and secure attachments to develop. Given this, it is significant that one child in three in the UK is likely to experience parental separation before the age of 16 (OnePlusOne). There will inevitably tend to be disruptions in living and educational arrangements as a result. In a secular society it is difficult, even tendentious, for governments or political parties to affirm marriage as an institution (by law or economic incentives), but the facts speak largely for themselves. There is evidence to suggest that parents living in stable marriages that are affirmed and supported by churches are statistically more likely to provide a more nurturing context for the development of their children.

There have been other changes in family arrangements over this period, including a tendency for more women to be in full-time employment, shared household tasks and parenting. The traditional image of a two-parent household with the husband as the breadwinner and the wife as the person responsible for the house, family and children is being replaced by more equal allocation of tasks and responsibilities.

One of the consequences is an increase of childcare facilities for pre-school children. Although extended families are more dispersed geographically than was the norm in previous generations, the role of grandparents in childcare is important practically and economically for many families.

Alongside these changes is the global shift in consciousness about children and childhood that can be identified with the passing of the United Nations Convention on the Rights of the Child in 1989. Children are increasingly seen as social agents, as fully human (as distinct from adults in waiting) and with inalienable rights that must be upheld by governments, if necessary against their parents.

Safeguarding and child protection are acceptable terms in public discourse that were rarely used prior to 1989.

The assumed rights of parents to bring children up in the faith to which they are committed has been challenged, for example by Richard Dawkins at the Chipping Norton Literary Festival on 21st April 2013, where he 'claimed that forcing a religion on children without questioning its merits is as bad as "child abuse" ' (Cooper, 2013).

Meanwhile, largely through market forces in neo-liberal capitalist societies, childhood has become commodified. Children are targeted as potential consumers and customers. And the advent of electronic communication means that this targeting can be continued 24 hours a day, largely outside the knowledge of parents.

Put together, this means that although the words 'house', 'family life' and 'household' are still used, the realities to which they refer have changed significantly, and perhaps in some respects out of all recognition. A family meal around a table without interruption by television, mobile phone or computer is becoming something of a rarity. Shared living, as in being together in the 'living room', is being replaced by separate activities made possible by multiple channels of television and options for communication.

Social relationships are increasingly shaped by the possibilities of networking using social media rather than mediated through parents and the family as a unit. Peer-group relationships have always been important in childhood, but they may have increasing significance in an age when geography and physical space are no bars to communication outside household or neighbourhood.

Meanwhile, changes in social life as a result of immigration mean that children in many parts of the UK tend to grow up and go to school alongside those of other languages, cultures and faiths. How the truth claims and traditions of a single faith – for example, Christianity – are transmitted and affirmed is changing. The majority of children in England do not attend church or Sunday school, and they will receive little Christian education at home or school. It may be that the children of evangelical Christian parents are therefore experiencing something of a countercultural childhood.

It is against this background that we consider the results of the surveys.

The surveys

The statistical material for this chapter comes mostly from two online panel surveys conducted in 2011 and 2012 and presented in the published reports. The former focused on families (*How's the family?*) and the latter on education (*Do we value education?*). The population of the two samples is not identical but is close enough for generalisations to be made across both. The respondents are churchgoing, committed evangelical Christians. (Only 1% were not attending church at the time of the 2011 survey. Ninety per cent describe themselves as evangelicals; 72% of households are 'entirely Christian', according to the 2011 survey.)

The size and composition of the households are not atypical of those more generally in the UK, with the exception that evangelicals are less likely to live in single-parent households (4%) than the national average (11%).

One household in eight has someone with a disability or care support needs. Of all the respondents, 142 described the nature of the disability or care with considerable openness and frankness, and the overall impression is of every human condition or frailty being present in one or more of the households. Evangelicals are not unacquainted with grief, and within their households and churches there is constant care and support going on across generations.

Marriage and divorce

At a time when cohabitation is becoming steadily more common in the UK, marriage is clearly valued highly by evangelical Christians. More than 80%, for example, have read a book about marriage, and nearly half (48%) have been on a marriage-related seminar or course. In the light of this commitment to marriage, it is not surprising that the percentage divorced is about half the national average.

Two-thirds of the adults (and 80% of the men) who responded are married, compared to 49% of the adult population in England and Wales (with a predicted downward progression to 42% in 2033). The average age of marriage among this sample is lower than the national average (men 25 rather than 31; women 24 rather than 28).

Of the respondents, 12.6% lived together before marriage. This is conspicuously lower than the national average of 75%. Faith status is connected with this in the minds of the respondents. Of those who lived together, 38% were not Christians when they got married, compared to 8% who were Christians when they married.

Eighty-six per cent of respondents grew up in two-parent families with their own birth parents, and 45% said that both of their parents were committed Christians. On the other hand, 31% come from homes in which neither parent was a Christian.

The connection between marriage and the Christian faith is evidenced in a number of ways, not least by the fact that 56% of the respondents met their marriage partner through a local church or a Christian group.

Predictably, more than two-thirds are strongly opposed to the changes in the law to legislate for same-sex marriages, and although the surveys were taken before the change in the law became effective, parents are aware that their children would encounter teaching contrary to traditional Christian values in their schools and among their peers.

Despite this commitment to the traditional understanding of marriage as a lifelong covenant between a man and a woman, there is evidence that the households represented are not immune to social trends such as rising divorce and cohabitation. Although 83% are happy with their marriage relationship ('fairly' or 'very'), there is evidence of stress within marriages, which many respondents were willing to identify. Twenty-nine per cent said they have sought help with problems at least once during their marriage over relationship, communication, sexual, infidelity or other issues. Comments included openness about emotional and physical abuse: this was a small minority, but indicative of the frankness of the responses of many participants. It must also be taken as a warning to churches to be alert to stresses leading to unacceptable behaviour in some of the families and households that regularly attend worship and other activities.

One consequence of the valuing of marriage is the existence of celibate singleness, which is countercultural. Twenty-two per cent of respondents are single, with 37% living alone. Not surprisingly, there is a gender difference here, with singleness more common among female respondents: 80% of men are married, in contrast to 58% of women.

In terms of the role of the church in supporting marriage, 95% would recommend marriage preparation. However, 40% or more received no marriage preparation from the church. This was especially so for the older generations. It is not clear from the survey what people had in mind when referring to 'marriage preparation', but as only 30% have experienced a 'multi-session course', it seems as if many may have had just one session with a minister or church leader.

While churches are seen by respondents to have a strong emphasis on marriage, there was an acknowledgement that churches are not good at teaching about issues of singleness, or offering pastoral support to those struggling with relationships. If a church is to advocate traditional marriage and sexual behaviour confined to marriage, then it is surely failing those in its congregation who do not find themselves in marriage covenants if it does not support them equally, or possibly with more dedication and concern.

Family

We turn now to the family or household (the *oikos* in NT terms). In the material and analysis that follows there are some questions lying in the background or beneath the surface. One concerns the degree to which the family/household sees itself and/or is seen by the gathered church (worshipping congregation) as 'little church'. A second is whether the church sees a role in supporting the household as a social group (as distinct from a collection of individuals of different ages that engage with the church and its activities). Third is how church sees itself – as a family or a household (the former is more prescriptive than the latter). Finally, there is the question of how far little family and church see those outside their domains and activities as their 'brothers', 'sisters' or neighbours in the sense described by Jesus in the parable of the Good Samaritan.

Family is important (the most important thing in life apart from God) to the vast majority of respondents (84%), and it is to the nature of these families that we now turn. Family life is changing in the UK because of a number of factors – sociological, economic and technological – and so the families represented in this survey reflect many of these changes.

In the 1960s, for example, only 22% of respondents experienced the mother in their household going to work while the children were growing up. In the current decade, in keeping with economic and social trends, this has risen to 37%. In the 1960s only 3% of children were cared for by childminders or in nurseries: this has now risen to 31%. In the 1960s the mother was responsible for almost all the childcare in the experience of 87% of the respondents; in the current decade this has almost halved, to 47%. There is a similar pattern with housework: from 88% where almost all was done by the mother/housewife in the 1960s, to 49% in the most recent decades.

More than 90% of those who responded believe that fathers should be fully involved in caring for their children. There is general agreement that children are at a disadvantage if there is no male role model in the household. At the same time, in the light of traditional biblical teaching on the roles of husbands and wives and men and women, there is a range of views on how far the husband should be the 'head' of the marriage/household, and whether the main role for women is in the home and looking after the family.

Economic pressures on families and households were referred to at different points in the survey (as we shall see), but when asked whether they are 'short of money', 36% said that their families were as their children grew up in the 1980s; 21% who were at that stage of life in the first decade of the twenty-first century; and 26% in the current decade. This broadly mirrors the experience of families in the UK over this period.

When asked what pressures Christian families face in today's world, there was continuous reference to economic pressure, including finance, the need to work, the difficulties of an appropriate work–life balance, and budgeting.

Grandparents have a significant role in the life of families, with more than 70% staying in touch with at least some of their grandchildren. The dispersal of families means that distance precludes contact for some, but there is an overall awareness of the importance of such relationships outside the immediate two-generational household.

Nurturing faith/Christian education

Households/little churches

Given the question of how far Christian households function as 'little churches', it is significant that 40% of respondents said that they pray daily together as a family. Between 21 and 33% said that they discuss family giving together, and more than half discuss global church and mission as a family. When it comes to reading the Bible together, it is clear that the days of Christian families reading the Bible together (and the days of Family Bibles) are no longer in evidence. Even where there are young children in the family, only 12-15% said that they read the Bible regularly together. Given the commitment of the respondents generally to the importance of the Bible as a guide and foundation to life, the assumption seems to be that reading the Bible together is something primarily done in the gathered church.

It may be that the faith background of the respondents helps to explain the comparative weakness of the 'little churches'. Fewer than 50% had two committed Christian parents during their childhood; one-third did not have any Christian adults bringing them up. So it is likely that fewer than half of the Christian parents grew up in households where specifically family Christian activities were common.

This is where the role of grandparents may be significant. More than 25% see themselves as having an important role in the Christian nurture of their grandchildren, and 45% said that they are sometimes involved in this. Is it possible that both churches and little churches have undervalued such a willing and very experienced resource?

Churches

Overall, 80% of the respondents said that their household goes to church together, although this figure is slightly less for those with children. The range of described activities for children and young people in their churches by the respondents was predictable: by far the most common are weekly Sunday school and youth church associated with Sunday worship. Regular weekday programmes and special events, parties and outings come second; residential camps or weekends away come next, and then joint events and activities with other churches. Training young people to be leaders (where the focus on organisations such as Christian Endeavour was once so strong), and engaging children and young people in overseas mission are comparatively weak.

There is awareness and engagement with some of the named Christian national groups whose focus is children and young people (Urban Saints, Youth for Christ, Soul Survivor, Scripture Union, Girls Brigade, Boys Brigade, Frontier Youth Trust, CURBS Project), but it is patchy. Scripture Union and Soul Survivor are the best known.

However effective the churches and these national organisations are at providing activities and resources for children and young people, it is not evident that they see supporting 'little churches' as an important function.

When it comes to assessing how far church and little church are effective in supporting the Christian faith of their children and young people, the picture is not particularly encouraging. Whereas the respondents rate highly the activities run by churches that are focused on children and young people, the data does not provide evidence that they are effective. For example, 45.5% of respondents agree that many young people stop attending church in their teenage years. There are 669 respondents who have children over the age of 11. Although 129 (19%) of them do not have children who are committed Christians, the remaining 540 claim to have produced a total of 679 offspring who are committed Christians. Assuming that each respondent is one of a couple of Christian parents, the biological replacement rate of committed Christians is only just over 50%.

When considering 'unchurched' children and young people in the vicinities of churches and little churches, there is, despite regular activities in some places, a comparative lack of enthusiasm and commitment. It does appear that the primary interest and focus is on the children and young people within the Christian 'fold'. Put another way, the decline in church attendance by teenagers brought up in Christian households is not being compensated for by the conversion of 'outsiders' (Griffiths, 2009).

Challenges facing Christian families today

One of the most revealing parts of the family survey are the comments of the 941 respondents who chose to answer the open-ended question about the biggest challenges facing Christian families today. The responses reveal considerable awareness of social trends and technological changes. These are people clearly in touch with the 'real' Britain of the twenty-first century.

It would be well worthwhile for churches and Christian organisations to take time to digest what these parents are saying before trying to explore the implications for the ministry and mission of church to today's children and young people.

One of the prevailing themes is the way in which families are surrounded by a culture of secular atheism that pervades every aspect of life, including schools, peer groups of their offspring, institutions and – crucially in an age of universal electronic communication – the media. Churches and little churches are implicitly conceived as being like Christian lights seeking to shine in a deepening darkness. It is obviously a post-Christendom era and non-Christian society in which they live and move and have their being. So deep thought and careful strategies are required to provide appropriate support for the next generation.

The responses could be read as an implicit plea for the help of churches and national Christian organisations to combine to support families and households in new and strategic ways. How can children and young people be given the resources to resist secular pressures without sustained Bible reading, for example? And what are the settings in which the next generations can share openly the challenges and pressures that they encounter in their daily lives? They find themselves in situations that are quite different to all their forebears (for example, in a society where the law on marriage has changed and their schools and the media will take for granted a non-traditional definition of the marriage covenant). Unless church and little church combine on this, and in radically new ways, what realistic hope is there for the faith of the future generation(s)?

The respondents are equally open about the individualistic, consumer-dominated, market-driven ideologies that dominate the society in which their children are growing up. This is the very air that their children (and their peers) breathe, often by means outside the parents' control, and beyond their knowledge. The message of the gospel – where love of God, self and one's neighbour go hand in hand; of relationships that have nothing to do with purchase or contracts; of love communities centred on the grace of God revealed in the loving sacrifice of His Son – is completely at odds with the spirit of the age. How should families live? How should churches model this alternative way of living?

The demands of work and the need for money to cover mortgages and the bare necessities of living mean that families find it increasingly hard to find ways of having quality time together, even on Sundays. How might church and little church combine to find ways of cooperating and sharing tasks in order to free up family times together? Is this where grandparents and single people in churches may have important, possibly irreplaceable, roles to play? It hardly needs to be said that neither grandparents nor single people live in a non-pressured world different from the one described by the respondents. But the situation is one that demands a corporate response: it may well take a village to raise children in the Christian faith in future.

If there is a willingness to heed the deep implicit warnings of the respondents, then the shape of church and little church may change significantly. Messy church, café church, liquid church, new ways of being church may all have their place. There is a genuine need for models of Christian community, not unlike mission stations and monastic orders in some respects (though not in others), where authentic expressions of Christian life and faith can be experienced.

Education

One of the most obvious and direct ways in which Christian children and their families interact in structured ways with the rest of society is through education, particularly schools, as well as in colleges and universities. For this reason alone it is valuable to have the views of parents and others in the churches on a range of aspects of education in the UK.

It is important to note at the outset that the views on education are informed by direct links between Christians, churches and education: this includes teachers, lecturers, etc. (20% of respondents) and those who have children at school or college (33%). In addition, many are enthusiastically engaged in further education or continuing study.

The educational background of the respondents is as follows: 72% attended a local state primary school; 14% a private school. Only a small minority went to a Christian school (7% or fewer depending on the era). Of those who went to state schools, 23% went to Christian voluntary-aided etc. schools, which is rather less than the population as a whole. Overall, this background is broadly comparable with the UK population as a whole.

When asked about the aspirations that parents have for their children's education, 48% talked of state or local comprehensive schools. The majority wish for some form of state-funded education (71%), with just 9% wanting a specifically Christian or home school. The primary consideration is the best-suited education for their children (92%), and 'the point of education' is seen primarily as that everyone should fulfil their potential as a human being (86%). Government outcomes such as equipping for working life and skilled workforce are seen as less rated by comparison (only 59% and 39% respectively see this as 'very important'). And Ofsted ratings (53%) are not as important as might have been expected.

Unsurprisingly, 64% want a school with a strong Christian ethos, and 58% a school where Christian beliefs are taught. But there seems to be a presumption or hope that a Christian ethos pertains in some state schools (other than Christian voluntary-aided schools). It also appears to be important that Christian children should mix with their peers rather than be in learning environments of like-minded people. This is clearly not so that Christian children should be squeezed into the prevailing ideological moulds: 93% see it as very important that children question the consumerism and individualism of today's society. It follows, then, that the need for churches, little churches and Christian organisations to equip children and young people with the Christian resources to withstand the pervading secular atheism that they will encounter daily becomes all the more relevant.

Conclusion

Although neither of the two surveys on which this chapter has been based was intended as an exhaustive or a comprehensive study of contemporary families, child-rearing and education, put together they do provide some significant information and pointers.

Overall is the impression of Christians with high ideals of marriage, family and church, and who are committed to the best for the next generation. These ideals are expressed within an understanding of some of the profound challenges that face Christian families living in a society whose prevailing assumptions and ideologies are at odds with many of those represented by traditional Christian beliefs and values.

Rather than retreating from such a challenging, even hostile environment, parents are seeking to prepare their children for citizenship in a contemporary world. They have confidence in the quality of the teaching and activities provided for their children. Whether this confidence is adequately founded in reality is open to question.

Given that there is a steady flow of teenagers away from formal church engagement, there is surely cause for thought. Hard-pressed parents understandably look to churches for the Christian nurture of their children and young people, but it is unlikely that this will be fit for purpose.

A much more robust relationship between church and little church is called for, and it could well be that Christian organisations can be catalysts for such a process.

References

Cooper, R., 'Forcing a religion on your children is as bad as child abuse, claims atheist professor Richard Dawkins', *Daily Mail* 22nd April 2013. Available at http://www.dailymail.co.uk/news/article-2312813/Richard-Dawkins-Forcing-religion-children-child-abuse-claims-atheist-professor.html (accessed 18th December 2014).

Ermisch, J. and Francesconi, M., *Cohabitation in Great Britain: Not for Long, but Here to Stay*, Institute for Social and Economic Research, University of Essex, 1998.

Ermisch, J., *Pre-marital Cohabitation, Childbearing and the Creation of One-Parent Families*, ESRC Research Centre on Micro-social Change, Paper Number 95–17, 1995, from British Household Panel Study.

Griffiths, M., *One Generation from Extinction: How the Church connects with the unchurched child*, Oxford: Monarch Books, 2009.

Haskey, J., 'Trends in marriage and cohabitation: The decline in marriage and the changing pattern of living in partnerships', *Population Trends*, Vol. 80, 1995, pp.421–29.

OnePlusOne, 'Evidence shows that the effects of separation on children can be limited'. Available at http://www.oneplusone.org.uk/content_topic/splitting-up/limiting-the-effects-of-separation-on-children/ (accessed 18th December 2014).

Response to chapter 6: Evangelical families, children and youth

Alan Charter

Those of today's emerging generation have been dubbed 'digital natives', reflecting their innate embrace of technology as part of everyday life. Those of us who have had to come to terms with these advancements ('digital immigrants') can often feel like we are playing catch-up. Importantly, though, it is a spur to us to recognise the cross-cultural investment needed to impart the gospel as we reach across the generations.

This presents challenges for us regarding faith formation, both in the church and in the home (little church), especially when considered against the current backdrop. Keith refers to 'a culture of secular atheism that pervades every aspect of life' and an 'obviously post-Christendom era and non-Christian society in which they live'. I am compelled to agree that 'deep thought and careful strategies are required to provide appropriate support for the next generation'.

Much good work exists in looking creatively at connections between church and home. The 'Sticky Faith' research from Fuller encourages a more thought-through approach to how faith passes from one generation to the next. The Global Children's Forum and other networks are encouraging a stronger formation priority.

One such example is the work done around Here2stay in Australia which acknowledges that a large part of our discipling strategy has revolved around the imparting of *information*. While curriculums and programmes are important, this strategy alone is not producing mature disciples; to do this we need to intentionally add experiences that focus on *formation* so that faith goes deeper. Such experiences are intended to encourage a child's faith to go deeper, to be more strongly rooted, and to provide a foundation and stability for the turbulent years ahead. They are explored through foundational formational experiences including Family nurture, Positive peer communities, Serving in mission, Peak experiences, Encounters with Jesus and discovering the big story of the Bible.

That 'the primary interest and focus is on the children and young people within the Christian "fold" ' suggests that many churches will only exist in ever decreasing circles.[2] It is exciting to see where churches and families are taking steps to address distinct needs in their communities. There is a growing movement to support children in care, through such organisations as Home for Good that seeks to find a home for every child who needs one. Many churches are involved with the Make Lunch initiative, supporting needy families through school holidays (The Cinnamon Network). At Christmas 2014, Scripture Union teamed up with two national foodbank groups to give 50,000 families a copy of a Christmas Bible comic with their festive food hampers.

Take confidence! As the church we must continue to look out into our communities to address the needs we find; to encourage parents in their role and then encourage them some more; to pay close attention to early years families to help them establish strong foundations; and to do all we can to join together church gathered (congregation) and dispersed (households), so that we mirror the pattern of God's people over the centuries to journey together to live and share faithfully from one generation to another.

> He ... established the law in Israel,
> which he commanded our ancestors
> to teach their children,
> so that the next generation would know them,
> even the children yet to be born,
> and they in turn would tell their children.
> Then they would put their trust in God
> and would not forget his deeds
> but would keep his commands.
> *Psalm 78:5-7*

Alan Charter is a field team leader with Scripture Union and Director of Children Matter!

---

[2] 'The massive missionary challenge posed by generations growing up without childhood involvement has so far not been met. The age structure of congregations today, and in particular the absence of children, therefore appears to have future decline already built in to it unless this missionary challenge can be met.' (Jackson, 2002:11).

References

'Sticky Faith'. Available at http://stickyfaith.org/ (accessed 31st December 2014).

Here2stay. Available at here2stay.org.au (accessed 18th December 2014).

Home for Good. Available at http://www.homeforgood.org.uk/ (accessed 18th December 2014).

Jackson, B., *Hope for the Church* (London: Church House Publishing, 2002).

Prensky, M., 'Digital Natives, Digital Immigrants'. *On the Horizon* (MCB University Press, Vol. 9 No. 5, Oct 2001).

The Cinnamon Network. Available at http://www.cinnamonnetwork.co.uk/cinnamon-projects/makelunch/ (accessed 31st December 2014).

Chapter 7: Evangelicals and the Charismatic Movement

Mandy Robbins and William K. Kay

The Charismatic Movement in Britain has an unexpectedly long history in the sense that the first post-war stirrings might be seen in the peripatetic life and ministry of David Du Plessis who, known as 'Mr Pentecost', attended World Council of Churches meetings in the 1950s and brought with him a warmth and mature spirituality (Harper, 1965:54–59; Ziefle, 2012). Before this, from about 1915 onwards, classical Pentecostal denominations had believed in, preached about and propagated spiritual or charismatic gifts (Randall, 1999:206–237). They had, however, been on the edge of mainstream life during the 1920s and 1930s even though their leading evangelists, like George Jeffreys, regularly filled the Royal Albert Hall with Whitsunday meetings or held campaigns that attracted the attention of the national press (Edsor, 1964; Cartwright, 1986).

Yet, for all their attempts to evangelise, Pentecostals were held at arm's length by both Anglican and nonconformist Christians. This was partly a matter of biblical exegesis since many evangelicals had accepted the dispensational or cessationist view that charismatic gifts were only present among the first generation of Christians as a divine boost to the founding of the worldwide church. Beyond this, it was clear that middle-class and educated evangelicals found the working-class and less-educated Pentecostals to be lacking refinement.

The usual dating of the beginning of the charismatic movement is associated with the outpouring of the Spirit at St Mark's Episcopal Church, Van Nuys, on Passion Sunday in 1960 (Harper, 1965:60). The Episcopal Church in the United States was known to be the best educated, the most refined and the most middle-class of American denominations. They really had nothing to do with the ebullient and coarse Pentecostals dotted all over the United States. When an Episcopal priest wrote to his parishioners saying that he had spoken in tongues, there was shock and distaste among his parishioners. The priest, Dennis Bennett, was moved to another parish and given a church that appeared to be ready to close for lack of attendance. Once

Bennett arrived, the congregation gained a new lease of life and grew rapidly. As a result, Bennett was featured in articles in *Newsweek* and *Time* magazines, and news of what was happening rapidly crossed the Atlantic.

So we may date the beginning of the charismatic movement in Britain to the early 1960s, and it is probably no coincidence that the movement is contemporaneous with the social change of the 'swinging sixties'. In Britain, the best-known charismatic was the evangelical Anglican, Michael Harper, who had been a curate at All Souls Langham Place under the tutelage of the well-respected star of evangelicalism, John Stott. Harper and Stott, though both Cambridge graduates, disagreed about what charismatic gifts entailed. Harper himself experienced 'baptism in the Spirit', left All Souls and set up the Fountain Trust in 1964 as an interdenominational support for emerging charismatics all over the ecclesiastical spectrum.

Thus we may note that the charismatic movement in the UK separated from, or came out of, classical evangelicalism. Stott remained an evangelical and essentially confined spiritual gifts to the early centuries of Christianity while Harper and other charismatics retained much of the doctrinal shape of evangelicalism but added a belief in tongues, prophecy, healing, visions and the like. The extent to which the charismatic movement was 'evangelicalism plus tongues' was later debated and, as time went on, the implications of believing strongly in the ministry of the Spirit were seen to create further distinctives which in the end made the charismatic movement diversify its praxis, as some of the findings in this analysis make clear.

Harper published and edited *Renewal* magazine and combined his vision for evangelical revival with renewal in the church. This renewal was to bring about a freshness in Christian experience as well as a new joy, hope and commitment to living as a follower of Christ in the modern age. It was, however, a vision that anticipated that the current ecclesiastical structures and hierarchies would remain in place. So the charismatic movement was not revolutionary: it did not threaten the bishops, cardinals, superintendents and archdeacons within the existing order. Their positions of authority would remain untouched. Only parish and congregational life would be revitalised.

The charismatic movement during the 1960s enjoyed signal success. Its big interdenominational conferences and music broke down existing barriers, with the result that it was possible to see Roman Catholics and low-church Protestants worshipping together, praying together, singing the same songs and expressing a common belief in Jesus. Yet during this period there were other more radical voices emerging.

One needs to go back to the ministry and writings of Arthur Wallis, originally a member of the Brethren, who received an experience of the Holy Spirit in the 1950s and as a consequence began to envision a simple, transformed, non-sacramental but spiritually empowered church (Wallis, 1991). One might say it was a Brethren vision coupled with charismatic gifts, itself a paradoxical idea since the Brethren had been among the most insistent upon J. N. Darby's dispensational theology. Wallis called together groups of like-minded men and began to outline his vision for the future, a vision that led to the starting of a number of popular summer Bible weeks where Christians took their caravans or tents for a grand week of holiday and evening preaching not unlike that which had been seen at Keswick since the nineteenth century. It was from such holiday gatherings that the restorationist message was first passionately preached.

In addition, we need also to recognise the voice of Martyn Lloyd-Jones – reformed, Calvinistic, radical and uncompromising. In 1966, at a meeting organised by the Evangelical Alliance, he issued a call for every evangelical to leave his or her existing domination and come out onto common ground to form a new pan-evangelical grouping (Kay, 2007:15; Atherstone & Jones, 2011).

When we combine the vision of Wallis and the vision of Martyn Lloyd-Jones and see how these visions conflicted with the renewalist vision of Michael Harper, it is evident that there would be a clash. Gradually, during the 1970s, a series of new restorationist groupings came into being (Walker, 1998; Kay, 2007; also see Percy, 1996, on Vineyard). Many of these people had originally come to a fresh experience of the Holy Spirit through the charismatic movement but had grown impatient with the consistent warnings about the dangers of divisiveness or 'rocking the boat'. These young leaders almost all held to a restorationist view of church history – that is, that the church, after the first century, had lost its way and descended gradually into dark ages by throwing away the reliance upon the Holy Spirit which had characterised the early apostles. They saw church history as being

139

a series of upward steps from the restoration of believers' baptism by the Baptists, to evangelical conversion among the Methodists and then Spirit-baptism among Pentecostals. The last step of this unfolding centuries-long history concerned the restoration of apostles and prophets equipped with charismatic gifts to found new New Testament churches.

These new churches were by and large more middle-class in orientation than the Pentecostal churches. Vineyard's activities in Britain had echoes of Anglicanism as Hunt (1995) shows. Some new churches, like Pioneer, had an ecumenical edge (Kay, 2007:340) while others, like Newfrontiers, were not especially interested in ecumenical activities. In the first instance they tended to be situated in the south of England, although the Bradford group associated with Bryn Jones was clearly northern, and Jones himself was unquestionably Welsh.

The same period saw extensive immigration to Britain from former colonies, and the settlement in many inner-city neighbourhoods, especially in London and the Midlands, of large numbers of Christians with family roots in the Caribbean and West Africa. Experiences of racism and rejection in the churches as much as in wider society, and according to some accounts a lack of spiritual fervour in the churches, led to the establishment of numerous independent churches. In most of these the forms of worship were strongly influenced by Pentecostalism, and many local fellowships became affiliated to international Pentecostal denominations such as the New Testament Church of God and the Church of God of Prophecy.

From the 1990s onwards, patterns of immigration became diverse, and the range of ethnic minority churches broadened. Some of the African heritage churches grew rapidly in numbers and have become the most thriving sector of urban church life in Britain. Again, they are largely Pentecostal or charismatic in ethos. Unfortunately, the size and demographic mix of our research samples and the limited space in this chapter do not allow us to analyse in detail the distinctive features of this stream of churches.

These new churches, described in detail by Walker (1998) and Kay (2007), formed themselves into networks rather than denominations and, as the years from the founding passed, they retained a distinct style which, in many instances, came to be copied by others. There was informality and yet belief in spiritual power, mission, miracles, speaking in tongues, home groups and the like.

The theology of the new churches is essentially restorationist and positive. They anticipate the growing power and influence of the church all over the world (and this may encourage them to political involvement), but their most obviously distinctive trait, in addition to belief in apostles and charismatic gifts, concerns the preaching of the kingdom of God. The 'kingdom' is a slightly ambiguous concept since it may refer to humanitarian or social justice issues or to non-denominational Christianity. For Bryn Jones, the preaching of the kingdom implied a sharp critique of apartheid (in the days before it fell) and a recognition of the rights of Palestinian Arabs. For others, the kingdom has been seen as the 'common ground' of Christianity upon which all Christians can stand, and is therefore implicitly an anti-denominational stance.

The current data will show to what extent beliefs about the kingdom of God held by this sample are also connected with a special concern for the poor. A simpler rationale for concern for the alleviation of poverty is found among Newfrontiers and other new churches in the direct apostolic exhortation to 'remember the poor' (Galatians 2:10). This emphasis has been taken to heart by Newfrontiers in relation to its work in South Africa, and genuine and successful efforts have been made to plant congregations in impoverished black communities. Alongside such beliefs is a strong commitment to mission. Such commitment requires regular congregational giving with the result that new churches, while they may be generous, may funnel their finance into mission projects selected by their leaders rather than into large, general and non-Christian charities. Moreover, in what at first appears contradictory, new churches may also hold a doctrine connected with the 'prosperity gospel' or the belief that God wills the financial prosperity of men and women, since poverty, from a biblical perspective, is a curse (Perriman, 2003). The blessing of the gospel cancels out the curse of poverty.

The data

The exploration of the data within this chapter is divided into four sections which explore some of the themes raised. The first section provides an overview of the charismatic groups. This includes demographic information and information on church attendance and the types of churches attended. The following three sections explore personal faith, attitudes toward issues within the UK (with a focus on education and work) and, finally, global issues. Each of these three areas is explored in comparison to attitudes expressed by those who do not assign themselves to the charismatic denominations detailed above. By focusing first on the personal domain, then the 'local' followed by the 'global', it is hoped that the exploration of the data will provide an insight into the different perspectives that charismatic participants hold across different areas of their lives, including the issues detailed above of engagement in humanitarian and social justice, and financial giving.

This chapter draws on data from five of the panel surveys in order to present a comparison between the new charismatic church groups outlined above and other evangelicals. Our standard question defining this category uses the wording, 'Charismatic – independent or non-denominational (e.g. Vineyard, Pioneer, Newfrontiers or local community church).' There may, of course, be a number of people among our respondents who would describe themselves as charismatic and who share the typical beliefs and practices of the new charismatic church groups but who attend churches of other denominations. However, none of the surveys contains questions that would allow identification of this subgroup. There is, however, a finding in the baseline survey to the effect that 86% of evangelicals 'disagree a lot' and 6% 'disagree a little' with the statement, 'I believe that the miraculous gifts of the Spirit (tongues, prophecy, miraculous healings, words of knowledge) stopped in the first century and are not seen today.' This suggests that cessationsim is now very much a minority view among evangelicals.

The first survey employed in this analysis is the *Life in the church?* survey. This survey enables us to present an overview of levels of engagement with church life together with a profile of the 324 people in the charismatic new church groups. This survey will underpin the first section of this chapter that explores the data. The personal faith section draws exclusively on the *Time for discipleship?* survey. The participants in this sample are 282 from the charismatic new church groups and 1,363 other evangelicals. The section that explores participants' attitudes to issues at home draws on two surveys: the *Do we value education?* survey and the *Working faithfully?* survey. There were 262 participants from the charismatic new church groups in the *Do we value education?* survey and 1,050 identified as other evangelicals. There were 298 participants from the charismatic new church groups in the *Working faithfully?* survey and 1,156 other evangelicals. The final section of this chapter focuses on participants' attitudes toward global issues. Here we draw on the *The world on our doorstep?* survey, with 213 participants from the charismatic new church groups and 891 from the other evangelicals.

The analysis employed to compare these two groups enables us to explore similarities and differences at a level that does not take into account other influencing factors beyond those implied by the headings. For example, the analysis only explores the basic differences between the two groups and does not tell us about the influence of factors such as age or sex.

Charismatics and church life

Of the 324 charismatic new church respondents who took part in the *Life in the church?* survey, 53% were male and 47% were female. More than a quarter (27%) were born in the 1950s, with the next largest group (22%) born in the 1960s; 15% were born in the 1940s, 14% in the 1970s and 13% in the 1980s. Overall, the age profile of the participants is clustered around the 40- to 50-year–olds, which suggests that they are younger than the average for our overall sample of evangelicals.

Weekly church attendance is high, at 86%, with a further 8% attending at least once a fortnight. A total of 94% are therefore attending Sunday morning worship at least twice a month. Attendance at other church services drops to one in ten or less. It is the Sunday morning service that is important to these groups. Three-quarters are committed to attending a home group or small fellowship group at least twice a month. Prayer meetings/groups are also supported, with more than half (55%) attending at least once a month.

The congregations the charismatics are attending tend to be of a healthy and viable size, with nearly a third (30%) attending a church with between 101 and 200 participants, and 15% attending a place of worship with more than 300 participants. The churches tend to be predominantly in small towns (33%) or city/large town centres (30%). Only 5% of the charismatics attend churches that are more than ten miles away from their home. More than two-fifths (45%) attend a church which is between one and three miles from their home, and more than a quarter (27%) attend a church that is less than a mile from their home. Given that the majority of participants live in urban areas, it seems that a distance of up to three miles from home can be seen as attending a church which is part of the local community. Half (50%) agree that their church comprises predominantly middle-class members.

The importance that this group of new church charismatics place on aspects of their church life demonstrates very little concern with the building itself (only 3% agree the building is important), the location of the church (only 6% agree a convenient location is important), the denomination of the church (only 4% agree that the denomination of the church is important), or a history of their own family ties to the 'place' (only 8% view this as important). This is a direct contrast to, for example, Anglicanism where a sense of place is perceived to be important (see, for example, the work of John Inge (2003) on a theology of place). What is important for this group is the quality of the interpersonal relationships within the church alongside teaching and services that inspire and build their faith. Thus, three-quarters (74%) agree that the quality of the relationships between members is important, 68% agree that the theological and doctrinal stance of the church is important, and 64% agree that the depth and relevance of Bible teaching is important for their personal growth. As one participant put it:

> The most important thing about a church is not how it does things in terms of format and liturgy, but whether there is reality in people's relationship with Jesus that makes a difference to their lives and how they relate to each other.

Although charismatic new church groups report high levels of satisfaction with their church and 74% agree that they are very happy with their church life at the moment, one in ten is not content. A similar proportion report that they have often thought about leaving and finding another church. But overall they are positive about their church, with three-quarters (76%) agreeing that their church is being shaped by a clear strategy based on an inspiring vision for the future.

With regard to outreach, 67% feel confident that they could invite a non-Christian to their church and that they would feel welcomed. A similar number (63%) feel that their church brings them into contact with people in the wider community. This perspective is supported by this participant who states:

> There is a big difference between what we perceive of church and what the reality is. We are told by the media that the church is in crisis, the church is leaking numbers and that it is out of step with society. However, the church is growing and God is moving in power across this nation.

This overview reveals a group of Christians who are worshipping regularly in large middle-class congregations usually within their local area. The quality of the relationships within their church community is of greater importance to them than the physical surroundings where they worship. They remain true to the roots of their movement and see themselves as being 'called out'; a vision for their church community is importantly based within a supportive structure of relationships.

The following three sections explore personal faith, local issues and global issues and present a comparison between the charismatic groups and the other evangelicals who took part in each of the panel surveys.

Personal faith

The focus in this section is on personal faith expressed through prayer. Ten areas were explored in the *Time for discipleship?* survey with regard to personal prayer. Personal prayer was explored by asking respondents how often they engage in specific prayer activity. The significant difference recorded between the charismatic new church and evangelical groups was frequency of listening to what God is saying, with more than a third (35%) of the charismatic groups stating that they engage in this when they pray compared to 27% of the evangelical group. One participant states:

> Spend time sharing with Father, what is concerning me and asking what He wants to do together with me each day – to give me His mind and share what He is feeling about situations and people. Asking Him to show Himself and lead my family.

Nearly a fifth (19%) of the evangelical group frequently 'ask God to work in situations overseas' compared with 14% of the charismatic groups.

The most frequent prayers by both groups are for their families, with just under half (43% evangelical and 42% charismatic) stating that they frequently ask God to bless their family. The next most frequent prayer by the charismatic groups is listening to God (35%). The remaining eight aspects of prayer cluster into two groups by frequency. Around a fifth to a quarter of the charismatic new church Christians frequently confess and seek forgiveness for their sins (28%), ask God to help or heal other people they know (24%), ask God to bless the work of their church (20%) and ask for people to come to faith in Christ (19%). Very few of the charismatic Christians frequently pray for healing of their own illnesses (6%), ask for help to overcome temptations (11%) or ask God to work in situations overseas (14%).

The data demonstrates that with regard to personal faith as explored by prayer frequency, charismatic and evangelical Christians are more alike than different. Out of nine possible areas that are explored, only one demonstrates a statistically significant difference – listening to God. Generally higher frequencies of prayer are more focused on issues that can be seen as of personal importance, such as family and church, rather than a concern with issues further afield. Both groups are least likely to pray for their own health and well-being: thus only 5% of other evangelicals and 6% of charismatics report that they frequently pray for their own healing.

Education

Two areas of attitudes to education are explored in this section based on the *Do we value education?* survey. The first considers what participants think should happen within school. The second explores what participants consider should be the purpose of education.

School content

The areas explored include discipline, extra-curricular school trips, uniform, collective worship, and science lessons. Two significant differences emerge between the two groups. First, charismatic Christians are significantly more likely to agree that the theory of evolution should be taught as the most plausible account of the origin of human life (62% compared to 46%). More than half of the other evangelicals do not agree with this view (54%). The evangelicals are also significantly more likely to agree that schools would work better if they could enforce discipline using corporal punishment (55% compared to 49%).

Across the other areas explored, there are no significant differences demonstrated between the two groups. For example, in both groups, a quarter (26%) agree that schools should not arrange trips or out-of-school activities that are too expensive for some families. A similar number agree that disruptive pupils should be excluded from lessons at an early stage (24%).

The purpose of education

The assessment of the purpose of education falls into three main areas. The first considers education in relation to the individual, the second in relation to society, and the third focuses on faith.

Of the five aspects explored that relate to what education should provide for the individual, four are statistically significant. The other evangelicals group are more likely to support these areas. For example, 68% of other evangelicals agree that a key purpose of education is to help everyone fulfil their potential as a human being compared with 61% of the charismatic groups. The same proportion agree with the statement that a key purpose of education should be to ensure that every person can think for themselves. Two-thirds (67%) of the evangelical group agree that a key purpose of education is to equip people for a successful working life, compared to 60% of the charismatic group. A similar proportion (65% compared to 58%) agree that a key purpose of education is to give everyone a rich cultural experience and interest in the world around them. The only response where the difference between the groups is not statistically significant is with regard to the item, 'A key purpose of education should be to help everyone to achieve high academic qualifications' (17%).

With regard to the purpose of education as being a benefit for society, those who are part of the charismatic group are significantly less likely to view education in this way. Nonetheless, 60% of those from the charismatic community agree that a key purpose of education should be to help build a healthy society where everyone is cared for and has a chance to contribute to the common good, and 60% also agree that a key purpose should be to value and treat people equally and respectfully. The percentage of agreement among the evangelical group rises to 68% for the first item and 67% for the second item. As one participant comments, 'Far more resources need to be expended on education of those with few life chances.'

Both groups express a similar level of agreement that a key purpose of education should be to direct human development towards God's objective for human beings to attain a godly character and act in a godly way (60% of other evangelicals and 58% of charismatics). Similar numbers agree that a key purpose of education should be to shape a worldview which corresponds to Christian values and biblical understanding (59% and 55% respectively).

For both groups, a social justice agenda becomes evident, with support for educational activities being equally open to all. There are strong levels of agreement with regard to the purpose of education, with high endorsement of items that put forward the case for education to promote a better society and good social engagement. This was articulated in the following way by one participant: 'Everyone should be encouraged to make the most of the opportunities given by education and be allowed to reach their potential. However, it must be recognised that no one path fits all.'

Work

In unpublished data from the 2013 employment survey, very little difference emerges between the two groups in their attitudes to the world of work. Overall, neither group has a favourable attitude towards employers, but they express a supportive view of the unemployed and those in low-paid jobs. It would seem that for both the charismatic and evangelical groups, their perception of the world of work is not positive and leaves much room for improvement in the way employees are valued.

Employers

Just over half of the charismatics (51%) and other evangelicals (52%) agree that most employers treat their staff fairly, but this, of course, means that a large proportion (49% and 48%) do *not* agree (or are not sure) that this is the case. This is summarised by one participant who states, 'I find work a great source of stress. There is one rule for top management and another for general staff.' More than two-thirds (67%) of both groups agree that these days people are expected to work harder for less money, and three-quarters (75%) agree that the wage gap between the top earners and those on a basic wage is too great.

Employees

There is a general perception among both groups that employees are hard-working and not necessarily benefiting in the way that they should from their hard work. For example, nearly half agree that many very capable women are trapped in low-pay, low-status and insecure jobs.

The charismatic and evangelical groups are supportive of those who are seeking work. Thus, 62% of the other evangelicals and 58% of the charismatics agree that most unemployed people would like to work but the system, or their circumstances, do not make a job easy to find or worthwhile once found. The great majority of the respondents do not agree that there are high numbers of skivers and scroungers who prefer to live on benefits rather than try to find a job: 83% of the other evangelicals do not think this is the case, as do 79% of the charismatics.

A significant proportion of both groups express concern at the lack of social justice within the workforce, both for those who are employed and those who are unable to find work. The social justice agenda comes through for both groups in their attitudes toward education and work. However, this is more pronounced among the evangelical group with regard to education. There are no differences in the two groups' attitude towards work. One participant commented, 'I have never heard a sermon about work in 41 years of church attendance. Why is this when many of us spend more time at work than anywhere else?'

Global issues

From *The world on our doorstep?* survey of 2012, a pattern seems to emerge when exploring how the two different groups engage with the global community. In broad terms, those in the evangelical group are significantly more likely to pray while those in the charismatic group are significantly more likely to engage in financial giving. Neither group is more likely than the other to be actively involved in local groups with a global agenda. One participant noted that completing this particular survey had 'made me think about my personal lack of support for other countries'.

One group of questions within *The world on our doorstep?* survey was concerned with individual activity in respect of global issues. Of the seven areas explored, the highest-endorsed item for both groups was prayer for Christians who are persecuted. Just under two-thirds (63%) of the charismatic groups said that they had engaged in prayer for persecuted Christians in the previous week compared with 79% of evangelical Christians. Those in the evangelical group are also significantly more likely to have had prayers in church for persecuted Christians in the previous week (65% compared with 38%). Perhaps this exposes a significant difference concerning the place of public intercessory prayer in charismatic as opposed to mainstream worship. Some charismatic fellowships simply do not do intercessory prayer in public worship, or if they do, it is random contributions from the congregation rather than led from the front. One participant noted that 'the weekly church prayer meeting will regularly have a mission focus based around the work of people we know'. Those in the evangelical group are also significantly more likely to have used a prayer letter or diary from an organisation supporting the persecuted church (50% compared with 37%).

Percentages drop within both groups with regard to the giving of their time to help the persecuted church. Thus 13% of the evangelical group reported that they had engaged in political action over the previous week, which dropped to 9% among the charismatics. In addition, 5% of the other evangelicals reported having volunteered their time compared to only 1% of the charismatics. Only one in ten of both groups reported having engaged in any activity on behalf of prisoners of conscience or oppressed groups who may not be

Christian. It seems that for both groups, those who engage globally tend to act on behalf of the global Christian community rather than the global community more broadly conceived.

The second set of questions in *The world on our doorstep?* survey explored the level of financial giving in which the two groups engage. Of the 15 areas explored, only three report significant differences. The charismatic groups are significantly more likely to have cut back on their financial giving because money is tight: more than a quarter (26%) of charismatics report that this is the case compared with a fifth (20%) of the other evangelicals. Those in the charismatic group are significantly more likely (66%) than the evangelical group (59%) to direct the majority of their giving to their church. The other evangelical group are significantly more likely (38%) to report giving a substantial amount when there is a disaster overseas, compared with 29% of the charismatic group. Overall, the data indicate that the evangelical group are more generous in their giving than the charismatic group.

For both groups, the actual involvement in groups that are championing global issues is low, with between 3% and 5% giving up their time to engage in such activities. However, many respondents actively support Fairtrade and Tearfund. Furthermore, some 45% of charismatics report that they have been on at least one short-term mission trip overseas, compared with around 30% for the other evangelicals in the survey.

Conclusion

The charismatic new church group and the evangelical group are similar on many matters of morality and social justice, but there are several significant differences revealed by the surveys. In keeping with their defining theology of the Holy Spirit, the charismatics are more likely to believe that 'listening to God' is an important aspect of prayer.

We were not able to distinguish between regular giving in the form of tithing and additional giving in the form of special offerings. Nor were we able to correlate levels of giving with annual or disposable income. Nevertheless, it is apparent that the charismatic new church groups funnel much of their giving through local congregations rather than to outside agencies. Indeed, some new church groups (Newfrontiers take this view) teach that parachurch structures are not to be found in the New Testament and should therefore be avoided. This emphasis on the local church, and especially one's own stream within the charismatic new churches, may also explain a weaker engagement in prayer with the wide range of persecuted Christians across the world.

Doctrinal concerns almost certainly drive attitudes to the theory of evolution. The other evangelicals are less likely to accept evolutionary teaching in schools (especially in respect of human origins), whereas charismatics have fewer qualms. We might say that this confirms the slightly fuzzier doctrinal position of charismatics over matters not central to their self-definition. Also, and in keeping with the traditional tough-minded attitude of evangelicals, there is a willingness to endorse corporal punishment in schools. Figures on this matter should be read carefully since they do not imply that the other evangelicals *want* to escalate corporal punishment but merely that they are more willing to support it than members of charismatic new churches. In any case, the latter group may represent a slightly younger generation than the other evangelicals.

Regarding education itself, both groups see this as having a value for society and the individual, although other evangelicals are more inclined to support the notion that education is intended to create autonomous human beings fulfilling their own potential and engaging in a successful working life. Again, the figures should not be misinterpreted since the difference between the two groups is, in percentage terms, relatively small.

Overall, there is evidence that doctrinal and experiential emphases have an impact on a range of social and educational issues. Although many churches do not customarily expound and apply their theology systematically or definitively, it is obvious that the cumulative impact of church teaching and ethos *can* measurably shift perceptions, attitudes, values and behaviours. It is not surprising therefore that charismatics in new churches are detectably different from many evangelicals on a number of metrics.

References

Atherstone, A. & Jones, D. C. (2011). *Engaging with Martyn Lloyd-Jones*. Nottingham: Apollos.

Cartwright, D. (1986). *The Great Evangelists*. Basingstoke: Marshall Pickering.

Edsor, A. (1964). *George Jeffreys: Man of God*. London: Ludgate Press.

Harper, M. (1965). *As at the Beginning: The twentieth century Pentecostal revival*. London: Hodder and Stoughton.

Hunt, S. (1995). 'The Anglican Wimberites'. *Pneuma, 17*, 105-118.

Inge, J., (2003). *A Christian Theology of Place: Explorations in Practical, Pastoral and Empirical Theology*. Ashgate.

Kay, W. K. (2007). *Apostolic Networks in Britain: New ways of being church*. Carlisle: Paternoster.

Percy, M. (1996). *Words, Wonders and Power: Understanding contemporary Christian fundamentalism and revivalism*. London: SPCK.

Perriman, A. (ed.) (2003). *Faith, Health and Prosperity*. Carlisle: Paternoster.

Randall, I. M. (1999). *Evangelical Experiences: A study of the spirituality of English evangelicalism 1918–1939*. Carlisle: Paternoster.

Wallis, J. (1991). *Arthur Wallis: Radical Christian*. London: Kingsway.

Walker, A. (1998). *Restoring the Kingdom* (fourth edition). Guildford: Eagle.

Ziefle, J. R. (2012). *David du Plessis and the Assemblies of God*. Leiden: Brill.

Response to chapter 7: Evangelicals and charismatics in 2014

Anne Dyer

The issue between these two groups has diminished over the past decade or more, as far as I can tell. Considering that both sides would accept Bebbington's four points of evangelicalism – conversionism, activism, biblicism, crucicentrism – we always end up on the pneumatological issues of praxis more than doctrine. Have churches noticed the work of the Holy Spirit in a greater way across the nation? I believe so. It depends on definitions, no doubt, but 'charismatic' worship styles have permeated many an evangelical conservative church. Healing services have a higher profile in a range of churches; spiritual gifts of prophecy, and visions and dreams are more acceptable. The African diaspora churches' contribution may have helped here, and even TV evangelists! Undoubtedly there are still issues and even accusations one to the other. The 'Prosperity gospel' has taken over as the divisive issue, over spiritual gifts.

According to Todd Johnson (2014:265–288), there are numerous types of Pentecostals/charismatics in the world today, proliferating more from the Global South than from the West (or North). From the research results of Kay and Robbins for the British scene,[3] we see five areas where they discerned some differences, and yet they are not that different.

Local church commitment

The higher commitment to relationships compared to buildings shows the first generational attitude of charismatics who are more mobile in their use of buildings to rent. Anglicans have had buildings for centuries and it is how to use them best that is the issue, but the

---

[3] It must be stressed that there are different connotations to the terms 'evangelical' and 'charismatic' with therefore different definitions in other parts of the world –particularly North America, for 'Charismatic' Evangelical, and again 'Classical Pentecostal'.

heritage is important to them. It is notable that geographically close to home churches are still important, and an understanding of 'place' may be an area for teaching for missional commitment.

Global mission

There seems to be a lack of evidence for concern globally among both groups, despite slightly more in the evangelical wing praying for agency organised matters or the persecuted church; the percentages are still low. The term 'missional' should also have permeated both groups by now. Here is another emphasis to work on for both. The global issues of interest for the charismatics are more on a 'local here' to 'local there' church basis, as seen in many a short-term mission from the charismatic churches. The charismatic church member's income levels and willingness to send short-term teams seem to indicate a different value system in the use of money and 'hands-on' work. Despite concern for the kingdom of God and the marginalised or the poor, it has not enhanced missional giving apparently; this again may mean that the 'local, micro' and 'further away, macro' level of understanding 'church' may be an area for charismatic churches to consider in their teaching. At least some among both groups are committed to mission globally, with both sending abroad and reaching out locally. Working together might use resources more effectively.

Anne Dyer is Senior Librarian and Lecturer at Mattersey Hall.

References

The National Association of Evangelicals, 'What is an Evangelical?'. Available at http://www.nae.net/church-and-faith-partners/what-is-an-evangelical (accessed 3rd October 2014).

Johnson, Todd (2014), *Pneuma*, Vol 36, issue 2. Available at http://booksandjournals.brillonline.com/content/journals/10.1163/1570 0747-03602006 (accessed 1st January 2015).

Chapter 8: Evangelicals and their global connections

William Ackah

Christianity is a restless faith. The gospel commission as outlined by Jesus in Matthew 28 to make disciples of all nations has meant that, since its inception, Christianity has been a moving faith that has gained followers wherever it has been planted. From its early first-century origins in Palestine, the Middle East, Asia and North Africa, the faith really emerged as a significant global movement with the arrival of first European nation states and latterly the USA as economic, political and religious superpowers. The history of the development of the faith from that of paupers, slaves and those on the persecuted margins of society to that of princes, kings and the establishment is a complex one that cannot be outlined in any great detail here, but there are themes that resonate from the history of the development and growth of Christianity that are inextricably tied to twenty-first-century evangelicals and their current global connections.

The emergence of Rome as a city state and then as a pagan superpower that conquered large parts of North Africa, Asia and Europe, including Britain, is well documented. The Christian faith that was born within that empire and how it went from being a persecuted and marginalised sect to being the dominant faith was remarkable. Equally remarkable, although less well known, was the Christian faith that would emerge out of the East, centred around Constantinople and further afield in places such as Egypt and Ethiopia. Theological disagreements and political rivalries in the early Christian era would result in the development of distinctive Christian churches in Greece, Syria, Egypt, Ethiopia, Russia and Armenia, among others, and seeing the faith spread to India, China and other parts of Asia. Many of the churches that emerged from the East took the title of Orthodox, but their emergence, growth and ongoing struggles over the centuries have been anything but.

In Western Europe, although the Roman Empire collapsed, the Roman Catholic Church which came of out of the empire was able to survive and flourish, and its fortunes were closely tied to the emergence of new nations in Europe who embraced and instituted Christian doctrines and practices as key aspects of the basis of their national identities. A key feature of the early European states which came to prominence in the latter part of the fifteenth century was exploration. This was based on around discovery, commerce and conquest. The Portuguese and Spanish were initially very prominent in this and, with the support of the church, they explored and conquered territory in Latin America and Asia and attempted to plant their faith there among the 'unbelievers'. Other nations would follow suit, including the British, Dutch, Danish and French, bringing an unholy trinity of enslavement, colonialism and Christianity to large parts of Africa, Asia and Latin America from the fifteenth through to the twentieth centuries. From meek and humble origins, Christianity became a conquering faith, bolstering the colonial expansion of Europe.

As stated, Christianity in its many guises and variations is inherently restless, so the faith that was represented by papal power and supported the divine right of kings, even as it moved abroad, was coming under pressure to reform itself within Europe. The Protestant Reformation challenged papal authority and the divine right of kings; it sought to return to making the faith accessible to the ordinary believer, and in so doing unleashed a wave of political, economic, social and intellectual reforms and reformations. These new ideas, alongside new forms of religious organisation and identification, also travelled outside of Europe, most notably to North America, where the ideals of individualised faith expression without compulsion were foundational in the establishment of the United States. The ideals of freedom and liberty also proved conducive in allowing new Christian denominations to come into being, ones that would have a renewed evangelical impulse both at home and abroad.

The history of Christianity from the Middle Ages reveals that it was Europeans and their descendants who were its dominant purveyors, shapers and missionaries. Christianity was able to assume a position as a global religion on the wings of European political and economic ascendancy, as European nation states expanded their interests across the world so the faith followed them initially as a Christian monolith in the form of Roman Catholicism. Later, as the notion of singular church declined and led to the establishment of multiple denominations and expressions of faith, so too did these faiths find expression in many parts of the world, riding on the wings of new missionaries.

The Protestant Reformation was a key instrument in the emergence of new forms of Christianity. Although the Christian denominations and forms that would emerge from it were many and varied, the emphasis of themes such as the priesthood of all believers, salvation by grace, the Bible and the Bible alone opened the door for communities of believers to have a more personal relationship with their God and a more equal relationship with their church leaders. These ideas would have a profound impact on the Christian faith and also on the wider European society and large parts of the world. Pietist traditions, most notably the Quakers, emphasising equality and social justice alongside personal morality, would have a powerful impact on thinking in the colonies of eighteenth-century North America. Other faiths such as the Moravians would also be influential, not only among enslaved Africans in the Caribbean but also in inspiring John Wesley, whose Methodist movement with its vigorous hymns, emphasis on personal and social improvement and mass open-air meetings would be an instigator of social and cultural change in England, North America and then across the world.

Alister McGrath in his important work *Christianity's Dangerous Idea: The Protestant Revolution – a history from the sixteenth century to the twenty-first* (2007:552) argues that it was sea power and the rise of the voluntary association that can account for the rise of evangelical Christianity as a global movement in the eighteenth and nineteenth centuries. As European powers engaged in enslaving, indenturing and colonising vast swathes of Africa, Asia and the Americas, so missionaries were able to enter these spaces, and the emergence of voluntary societies provided the mechanisms for them to do so. For example, the late eighteenth century saw the establishment of the Baptist Missionary Society and the London Missionary Society, both supporting the spreading of the gospel overseas and laying the foundations for the establishment of churches, schools and medical missions in many parts of the world. These were spaces where many future leaders of independence movements in Africa, the Caribbean and Asia would receive their introduction to the positive moral, ethical and spiritual dimensions of the faith, and also its contradictions.

Even in the period of enslavement and colonialism, evangelicalism was not a monolith with a single trajectory and destination, slavery in the Americas being a clear case in point. Evangelicals were at the forefront of the abolitionist movement in Britain in the eighteenth and nineteenth centuries, and some denominations like Methodists and Baptists were converting enslaved Africans to the faith in the Americas, and by so doing contributed to making the system untenable. At the same time, some church ministers and churches were profiting from enslavement and using the Bible to justify the evil practice. However, ultimately the faith inspired opposition to enslavement encapsulated in songs, protests, revolts and votes which led to its demise, and has resulted in very vibrant forms of Christian experience in the Americas which have been culturally, politically and socially influential in North America, the Caribbean and, to a lesser extent, Europe.

These were not the only forms of Christianity in evidence during the era of Europe's rise. Christianity, as we have outlined, is inherently restless and so was manifest also in Africa and Asia in this period by the people of the continents. The faith appealed to the powerful and the powerless, to the rich and the poor, to the coloniser and the colonised, and this should not be forgotten even in an era that was primarily characterised by European nation-state power.

The rise of the United States as a global superpower in the twentieth century has coincided with profound shifts in political, social and economic forces around the world, and Christianity has also undergone major change in this era. As outlined, part of the ethos of the USA was its desire to be a nation free from the tyranny of kings and the alignment of religion and political power. Out of the many outcomes that stemmed from the USA emphasising individual liberty, freedom of worship and democracy was religious revivalism and the emergence of new ways of practising Christianity that were different from the formalism of faith that had dominated in Europe, such as Catholicism and Anglicanism.

One of the powerful new forms of faith that emerged out of what came to be called the Great Awakening of the nineteenth century was Pentecostalism, a vibrant form of evangelical Christianity that was birthed in this new environment which then exploded across the world in the twentieth century. Pentecostalism, although not the only expression of religious revivalism in the nineteenth century, was the most pronounced. It has been part of a process of change that has shifted the numerical centre and focus of Christianity away from Europe to Africa, Latin America and Asia. The trajectory of the faith has moved from being principally of white Europeans as its leading protagonists and adherents to being a faith of people of colour from most parts of the world.

The freedom and liberty emerging from the US political and economic sphere, and undoubtedly influenced by religious ideals and thoughts, has also had a profound impact on where and how Christianity is practised and who could practise it. Rather than the traditional church with trained and ordained clergy being the only sanctioned place where the faith could be practised, now shops could be churches, tents could be places of worship, warehouses could be sanctified spaces, and anyone who could demonstrate that they were filled with the Holy Spirit could lead a group of believers. The opening of the Christian religious space in the nineteenth and twentieth centuries to new people, new places and new ideas is part of a broader trend taking place around the world, which has seen the increasingly rapid movement of people, goods and ideas around the globe. Although not a new phenomenon, advanced technological developments mean that it has never been easier for goods, services, ideas and people to move. While this is often referred to as globalisation, some academics prefer the term transnationalism to refer to the increased movement of people around the world and their living in multiple spaces and places throughout their lifetimes.

The US has a been a prime mover and beneficiary of globalisation, with McDonald's, Coca-Cola and Hollywood movies being ubiquitous across the globe, but it has not been the only beneficiary: global processes are inherently restless, and what moves across the globe and whether it takes root in different countries and localities is by no means a given. In addition, the flow of goods, people, ideas and cultures is not a one-way process. Products, people, ideas and cultures flow into the US and other developed economies as well as to the so-called 'developing world' – Christianity being a powerful example of this. Evangelical Christians have embraced new technology and have utilised it to spread their faith across the globe. Hence many US-based denominations and individual ministers broadcast across the world through televangelism programmes, they utilise the internet to spread messages across the globe and have physical presences in the form of churches in many countries.

Evangelical Christians are involved in the music industry, making Christian films and other forms of media and entertainment for domestic and international audiences. This is not a one-way process either: Christians from Africa, Asia and Latin America are also developing physical and multimedia ministries that are distributing Christian messages in Lagos, Seoul, Mumbai, Amsterdam, New York, Atlanta, London and other urban centres across the globe.

A good example of how globalisation has assisted in changing the locale and centres of Christian influence comes from Australia. The songs of a church based in the suburbs of Sydney – a place not previously known as a centre of Christian thought and practice – are now sung by Christians all over the world, enabling Hillsong to become a global brand and an influence on global Christianity.

So the location and focus of Christianity is changing as a result of globalisation and transnationalism. Nations, too, are changing as a result of these processes, Britain being a powerful example. At its zenith in 1922, the British empire covered about a quarter of the world's land and ruled a fifth of the world's population. British influence and imperial power stretched across vast areas of Africa, Asia and the Caribbean, and so too did the Christian faith with missionaries, churches and schools existing to varying degrees in the empire. Hence the Anglican *Book of Common Prayer* and the Methodist hymn book could be as well known in the Gold Coast (now Ghana) as they were in Britain.

Move forward to the year 2000, roughly 100 years. Britain has experienced two world wars, its empire is no more and the country and its institutions have had to change from being an imperial power sending its people to rule in different parts of the world to being one nation among many in Europe, opening its borders to receive people from all over the world in order to help its economic growth and development in the era of globalisation. The people who have come to Britain, from Africa, Asia and the Caribbean in the aftermath of the Second World War, and more recently from Western and Eastern Europe and other parts of the world, are transforming the cultural landscape of the country, including its Christian landscape. Some have brought with them a Christianity of the *Book of Common Prayer* and Methodist hymn book, while others have brought faith that is more rooted in their own cultural, social and political experience.

The impact of this change is still being played out in the political, economic, cultural and religious life of the nation, and this is reflected in the survey responses of the political, economic and international outlook of evangelicals in Britain in the twenty-first century.

Mission, and mission in reverse

Evangelical Christianity in the UK continues to hold a global vision and international mission consciousness, and for many this goes beyond prayer into the giving of time and money. In *The world on our doorstep?* survey, which was completed in February 2012 by 1,151 respondents, we discovered that 42% have been involved in some form of Christian mission or aid and development activity overseas.

This figure of 42% includes 5% who have done long-term overseas service of more than two years, and a further 5% who have done medium-term service (between three months and two years). A further 20% have been on a single short visit of up to three months, and 13% have done this more than once. Charismatics appear more likely than average to have done one or two short trips, and the middle-aged group (35–55) are the least likely to have done any such trips. Presumably this is because younger and older people have fewer financial, work, family and other responsibilities. A little more than 25% are planning a short visit in the next couple of years, and 4% are considering offering for medium- or long-term Christian service overseas. Charismatics and Pentecostals appear most likely to plan a short trip (36% and 39% compared with the 25% average). Also, the under-35s are more likely than average to be planning this (33% compared to the 25% average).

There is an overwhelming commitment in principle to global evangelisation. A total of 71% strongly agree, and 27% agree that God still wants the church in the UK to be active in world evangelisation. Evangelicals believe the task is still unfinished: 62% strongly agree and 34% agree that there is still a lot to be done before the Great Commission is fulfilled and the gospel is proclaimed to all the nations. Many are committed to prayer for this:

- 50% say they have prayed for a particular missionary, church, mission or project overseas within the last week and a further 31% within the last month;

- 32% say they have used a prayer letter or diary sent by an organisation working overseas within the last week, and a further 29% within the last month.

When asked, 'Which of the following regions should be the highest priority for your church's mission, prayer and support? (Tick up to three)', 68% mentioned the UK followed by 48% mentioning Africa, 41% the Middle East/Islamic countries and 28% Asia. Europe came next with 20%, and Latin America received only 11%, with minimal mentions for North America and Australasia. These figures seem to suggest that despite general support for world mission, in most people's minds Britain comes first. The focus on Africa may suggest that compassion, aid and development may be more salient than evangelism. Likewise, we can suspect the high priority given to the Islamic world may reflect concerns for world peace and news coverage as much as real commitment to evangelistic mission.

Christians in the UK believe they can be inspired by and learn from the church abroad. For example, 74% of our respondents think we need missionaries from other countries to come and bring the gospel to people in the UK. This was nicely captured in the 2012 BBC TV series *Reverse Missionaries*.

Our respondents' churches also seem very committed to the global church. Almost all pray for international situations, and more than 75% of our panel belong to churches which have a significant relationship with at least one other church or Christian project in a foreign country. Generally, larger churches are significantly more likely than smaller ones to have a range of groups and activities. In almost all cases, females are more likely not to take part or to be unsure about what is on offer in their churches.

Global poverty and injustice

Our surveys show that evangelicals (alongside many other Christians) are in the forefront of concern and action to tackle world poverty and global injustice:

- 91% agree or strongly agree that we need to continue to campaign hard if we are to make poverty history; 82% agree or strongly agree that the international system of banking and trade is unfair and the poorest people in the world suffer as a result;

- 75% agree or strongly agree that the international arms trade is immoral and should be stopped;

- 56% agree and 9% strongly agree that the UK government has a good record of providing financial aid to the poorest countries in the world, amounting perhaps to an acknowledgement that the UK is not doing badly but might do better;

- 56% agree or strongly agree that it is not acceptable for this country to benefit economically from trade with undemocratic regimes;

- 64% understand the connection between the environment and poverty and agree that unless we act to reduce global warming, many of the poorest countries will suffer major disasters in the next 100 years.

There was perhaps more uncertainty over the statement, 'UK overseas aid should not go to countries with a poor record on human rights': more than 35% disagree and 40% are unsure. However, this can be interpreted as a generous opinion which for many respondents may be seen as endorsing the idea that in spite of oppressive governments we should still continue to aid the poorest people in those countries through local church and community projects.

Surprisingly, on the statement, 'The rise of China, India and Brazil is a good thing for the world as a whole,' 38% agree compared with only 7% who disagree, with more than half uncertain.

Are we good neighbours?

From the results of our February 2014 *Are we good neighbours?* survey, there seems to be little feeling of restricting charitable giving to either home or overseas causes, implying that we should give equal priority to both, although younger people born after 1980 are more likely to prioritise near at home.

Just under half are involved in three key activities linking with our neighbours across the world:

- 55% by ethical consumerism (fair trade etc.)
- 46% by prayer support
- 43% by child sponsorship

Which issues or social groups in overseas countries should Christians from the UK be making a priority in 2014, through church initiatives, international development organisations or campaigns?

- Poverty 19%
- Trafficking 18%
- Persecuted church 9%
- Syria 7%
- Fair trade 6%
- Clean water 4%
- Children 4%
- Women 3%
- Climate change 2%

In general, then, we see that evangelicals have a generous internationalist orientation, strongly in favour of justice, peace, human rights and the care of creation. There are few signs of an uncaring attitude or of a desire to dominate other less-fortunate nations. There may be less certainty on the practicalities of policy, and this orientation

Graph 8.1 Are you involved personally in any of the following international activities: *Are we good neighbours?* survey (N = 1,497 evangelicals)

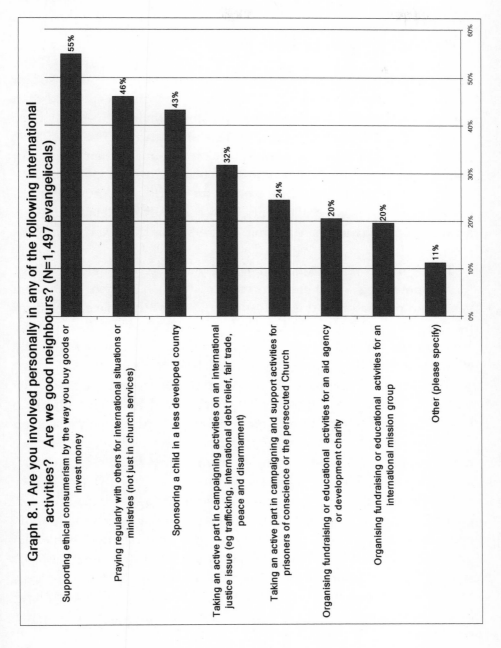

Graph 8.1 Are you involved personally in any of the following international activities? Are we good neighbours? (N=1,497 evangelicals)

- Supporting ethical consumerism by the way you buy goods or invest money — 55%
- Praying regularly with others for international situations or ministries (not just in church services) — 46%
- Sponsoring a child in a less developed country — 43%
- Taking an active part in campaigning activities on an international justice issue (eg trafficking, international debt relief, fair trade, peace and disarmament) — 32%
- Taking an active part in campaigning and support activities for prisoners of conscience or the persecuted Church — 24%
- Organising fundraising or educational activities for an aid agency or development charity — 20%
- Organising fundraising or educational activities for an international mission group — 20%
- Other (please specify) — 11%

may not always be converted into active campaigning. It is probably the result of long-term exposure through churches to the work and campaigning of international development agencies such as Tearfund, Christian Aid and World Vision.

Religious liberty and concern about persecution

Followers of Jesus should not be surprised if they are despised or persecuted. Indeed, there has been some concern expressed that Christians in the UK are not as free to express their faith as they once were, and a number of high-profile cases where Christians have alleged discrimination in the workplace on account of their religion or beliefs. However, little, if any, of this can be described as 'persecution'.

But in numerous countries around the world, the persecution of Christian believers is a daily reality. How far are evangelicals in the UK aware of and active in supporting the persecuted Church around the world?

The short answer is that awareness seems to be very high (90% have heard something about persecuted Christians in church in the last year), and prayer support is widespread (78% say they have prayed for persecuted Christians within the last month). North Korea, Iran, Pakistan and other countries in the Islamic world are most frequently cited as places where persecution of Christians takes place.

It is interesting that most people will pray for the persecuted church while 80% have not volunteered their time and 57% have given no money in the last year to an organisation supporting the persecuted church. Only 22% have been actively involved in regular prayer meetings, groups, activities or fundraising efforts (with a further 20% aware that their church runs such activities).

On the other hand, 91% agree or strongly agree that, 'The UK government should speak out more strongly on issues of human rights and religious liberty in countries with oppressive regimes,' while just under half have 'taken political action (such as emailing an MP, signing a petition) on behalf of the persecuted church' in the last year to raise concerns. A much smaller number (28%) have done something to support prisoners of conscience or oppressed groups who may not be Christians.

The multicultural church or the ethnic church

Over the last 50 years the UK has become a much more diverse and multicultural society, as a result of immigration. Immigration has also brought religious diversity, both in the presence of non-Christian faith communities and in the growth of churches where the majority of worshippers are from ethnic minority backgrounds. Significant numbers among them are evangelical and Pentecostal. In our survey we wanted to find out how far the evangelical constituency as a whole is aware of and in touch with this diversity, and the impact this is having on church life.

The vast majority of our panellists have a positive view of immigration and diversity and the contribution recent migrants have made to the church. There is little evidence of racism or xenophobia on a widespread scale. For example, 54% agree and 18% strongly agree that 'immigration has led to a vibrant diverse society in the UK'. The proportions are significantly higher among women, younger people and those who have family roots outside the UK.

Roughly the same number support the statement, 'The Church in the UK has benefited greatly from the contribution of immigrants over the last 50 years', and the proportion agreeing strongly rises to 21%. For this statement there is no age difference and it is the men who are most likely to agree.

Many government statistics estimate that the number who are not of white British heritage lies between 12% and 20%. However, a third of our respondents believe that more than a quarter of the national population falls into this category. At the more local levels there is a wider variation, depending to a large extent on where the respondent lives and the well-documented patterns of diversity in different regions of the country. People from London, the West Midlands, Yorkshire and the north west of England tended to estimate higher than average and those in south-west England, north-east England, Scotland and Wales the lowest. Almost 40% of our panel reported more than 5% of such people in their church congregations, almost identical to their estimate for work colleagues or fellow students. Along with regional and age differences, denomination seems to make a difference, with Pentecostals, Baptists and charismatics more likely than average to have larger proportions of minorities, and respondents from the Church of Scotland least likely. People with family roots beyond the UK were also likely to report higher proportions.

Of those born outside the UK, 14% attend a church where more than half the congregation come from an ethnic minority, compared with 5% for the UK-born. These figures provide very little support for the idea that evangelical churches exclude minorities or are segregated by ethnicity to any greater degree than localities, though there is some evidence from beyond our surveys that some minority groups continue to cluster together to worship with others from their own cultural backgrounds.

Similar patterns can be found for questions focusing on friendship circles, close friends and family ties. However, 49% of respondents have fewer than 5% of people from minority backgrounds among their wider circle of friends and acquaintances, while the figure rises to 70% for close friends and 80% for extended family connections. Those who reported the highest proportions of minorities in their locality and among their social networks are based in ethnically diverse areas such as inner London boroughs or Birmingham. This pattern is confirmed in data from the *Are we good neighbours?* survey of February 2014. In this, friendships are most commonly restricted by ethnic group in that 15% have no friends of a different ethnic background, with people living in Northern Ireland, Scotland, Wales and south west England more likely to have all their friends of same ethnic group. On the other hand, substantial numbers (45%) think monocultural neighbourhoods are a bad thing.

There is some very interesting data about elements of personal identity which can be directly compared to a nationally representative sample of the public in the 2009–2010 *Citizenship Survey*. Evangelical Christians are far more likely to place high importance on their religion and far less likely than the general public to find a sense of who they are in their ethnic or national origin or in social class, occupation or income levels.

Graph 8.2 Sense of who you are – very or most important. Comparison with national sample in *Citizenship Survey* 2009–2010.

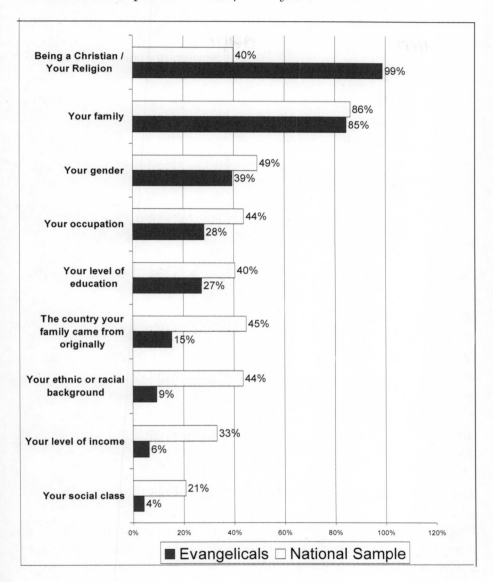

Table 8.1 Sense of who you are – very or most important. Comparison with national sample in *Citizenship Survey* 2009–10

	Very or most Important	Quite important	Very important	Quite important
Your social class	4%	27%	21%	39%
Your level of income	6%	42%	33%	43%
Your ethnic or racial background	9%	28%	44%	33%
The country your family came from originally	15%	32%	45%	34%
Your level of education	27%	46%	40%	42%
Your occupation	28%	39%	44%	28%
Your gender	39%	34%	49%	33%
Your family	85%	12%	86%	11%
Being a Christian/your religion	99%	1%	40%	22%

The encounter with other faiths: local religious diversity

In *The world on our doorstep?* survey we asked respondents to assess religious diversity in their local neighbourhoods. It is striking how much our evangelicals see themselves as in a lonely minority: significantly more than half (57%) think fewer than 5% of people around them are committed Christians. There are some regional differences, with people from Northern Ireland likely to estimate the highest proportions, while those in south east England, East Anglia, the East Midlands, Yorkshire and Scotland estimating lower than average.

Graph 8.3 Indications of local and national identity. *Are we good neighbours?* survey (N = 1,497 evangelicals)

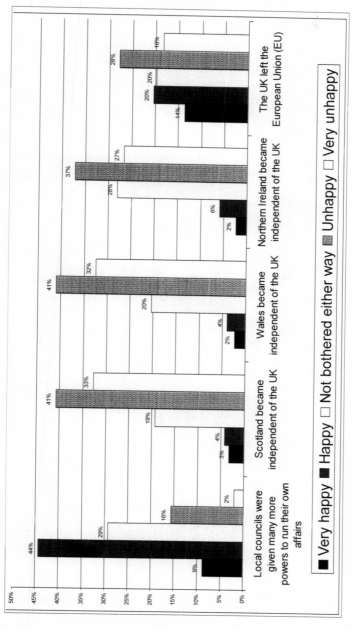

Graph 8.4 How important are each of the following to your sense of who you are? *Are we good neighbours?* survey (N = 1,497 evangelicals)

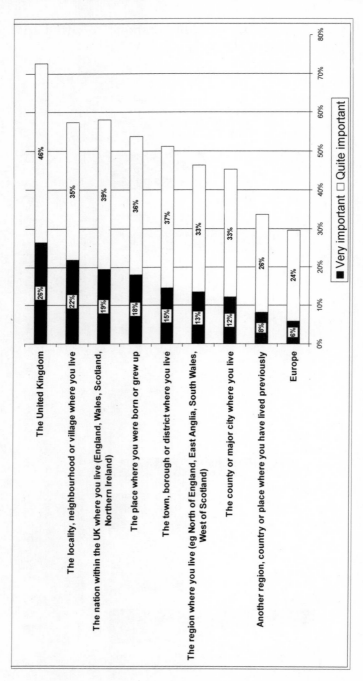

It is quite surprising that respondents appear to see themselves as surrounded by greater proportions of atheists and agnostics than of nominal Christians. Of our panel, 57% think that more than 25% of people in their local area are of no religion, and 28% think that more than 50% are. There is a mismatch here with national statistics. The British Social Attitudes survey of 2007, for example, shows that 47.5% identify themselves as Christian (although only 12% claimed to belong to a church), while in the Census, the basic religious affiliation counted 72% as Christian in 2001, falling to 59% in 2011.

For minority religions, the perceptions of our panel appear more plausible – more than three-quarters believe that Muslims account for less than 5% of their neighbourhood population and more than 90% that Sikhs, Hindus and Jewish people are in similar tiny minorities. The estimates were higher among people living in London and the West Midlands and among under-35s. The fact that these estimates identify the non-Christian faiths as small minorities in most localities where evangelicals live offers little support for the suggestion that our country is being 'taken over by Muslims (Sikhs and Hindus)'. In fact, there appears to be a surprising level of positive acceptance of Muslim neighbours – for example, half agree and 23% strongly agree with the statement, 'Christians in the UK should see their Muslim neighbours as friends and allies rather than the enemy.'

There is a general uncertainty about the prevalence of racism in the church in the UK. Around 23% agree or strongly agree with the statement, 'There is an unacceptable level of racism in the church in the UK', compared with 34% who disagree or strongly disagree and 43% who are not sure.

Views on nationalism and Europe from *Are we good neighbours?* survey

These graphs suggest that UK/British identity is important to a large majority of our evangelical panellists while European identity is not, and that a slight majority are pro rather than anti membership of the EU.

Multicultural mission and ministry

How far are evangelical Christians engaged in mission and ministry that touch minority communities? The short answer from our panel is, not much and not enough. Only a third of churches (and one in five individuals) are involved in evangelism or community service that touches these communities, and the level of involvement in training, partnership or interfaith networks is lower still. People in London and Yorkshire reported higher levels of involvement. There are also age differences, with over-55s more likely to be involved in evangelism and community service but less likely to be involved in partnership, interfaith networks or awareness training. This possibly suggests a more nuanced and less confrontational view of mission among younger people.

However, detailed breakdowns suggest that the level of engagement rises for those who live in areas of substantial minority settlement. For example, where the local population of minorities is thought to be between 25% and 75%, the proportion of churches involved in evangelistic outreach rises to more than half, and of individuals involved to more than one in three. More encouraging are the detailed, open-ended answers from more than 270 of our respondents, documenting a wide range of community engagement and outreach activities that do indeed make contact with people from ethnic and religious minorities:

> Evangelistic outreach and community activities are not targeted at minority ethnic/religious groups, but most certainly include/serve them as a matter of course.

> There is a Pakistani Christians group using the church and ESOL classes for members of this community. There is a mosque within the church's area and there is dialogue between local ministers and other faith groups.

> I am a prison chaplain where we have a diverse cross-section of prisoners and chaplains from a variety of world faiths.

Befriending the Somali community and other minority ethnic groups. Offering practical help to minority ethnic groups through local project. Alpha for Chinese students.

Northern Ireland is not particularly diverse, especially where I live; however, there is an increasing Polish community which I work with through my job as a trainer working in health and on local community projects.

I work for a Christian charity which serves destitute asylum seekers.

We have a Near Neighbours Worker and attend Christian/Muslim forums, interfaith Birmingham forums and training sessions when possible. We support asylum seekers and Christian workers globally – prayer/financial. I work for two congregations; both contain people of widely diverse backgrounds and cultures.

Questions of war and British intervention

Christians have long been divided between those who are pacifists at heart and those who believe that a just war is sometimes necessary as the lesser evil. There are also differences in particular cases in deciding whether a war meets the criteria around justice and political necessity. Our survey sought to gain insight into evangelical opinions on instances in which the UK government has intervened in conflicts using military force. Our survey reveals a slight majority in favour of the 2011 intervention in Libya, a slight majority against the involvement in Afghanistan and less than a quarter feeling that the invasion of Iraq in 2003 was justified: some 45% believe it was wrong.

The differences in opinion regarding the rights and wrongs of the three conflicts vary significantly in terms of age and gender of the respondents. Half of under-35s and 48% of women are not sure what they think about the Afghan conflict. The response to the Iraq conflict is similar, although graduates are more likely to be opposed than people with fewer qualifications. Older people are more likely to be against armed intervention in Libya, and under-35s are more likely to be in favour or unsure.

War and peace

Table 8.2 Do you think the UK should have taken military action?

	Yes	No	Don't know/ Unsure
In Afghanistan (2001)?	29.0%	33.2%	37.8%
In Iraq (2003)?	22.5%	45.4%	32.2%
In Libya (2011)?	35.4%	31.2%	33.4%

Reflections and conclusions

The survey data reveals that overall, evangelical Christians are adapting well to the dynamics of globalisation and transnationalism and the impact they have had on Britain. The vast majority of the survey respondents (more than 90%) would define themselves as white British, but their responses suggest an increasingly international outlook. The United Kingdom has a long history of ethnic diversity spanning centuries, but the post Second World War period has resulted in more people than ever before from different parts of the world making this country their home. Evangelical Christians seem to have broadly accepted these changes and welcomed the positive impact that this has brought to churches and the wider society.

There is in the data, however, still a sense that there is a difference between minority and majority ethnic experience, and that evangelicals 'do work' in minority communities as opposed to being an integral part of those communities. One of the striking facets of globalisation is the degree to which an international or global issue is a local, or glocal, issue at the same time. So the plight of Muslims in Syria or Palestine is not just an issue in the Middle East; it is also an issue in Tower Hamlets in London and in Glasgow in Scotland, whereby people will show their solidarity, give resources and in some cases even their lives, so closely do they feel attached to the people and places where their brothers and sisters in the faith are suffering.

The data suggests that although evangelicals place a high value on their Christian identity and have in many cases engaged in missionary activity abroad, the depth of that identification across national boundaries to embrace and support Christian brothers and sisters of different cultures and ethnicities is not deep enough. There is room for the evangelical community in Britain to think more deeply and conceive of itself more broadly as part of a global family and to consider what its responsibilities are as part of a family, not as its head as in times past when Britain 'ruled' the world, but as an ordinary member of a global community, concerned about what happens to family members and strangers wherever they are in the world.

Part of the responsibility of being part of a global community as identified by the survey is the role that churches play in issues of global poverty and injustice and of persecution. It is positive to see from the responses that evangelicals are aware of these issues and are willing to put resources in and lobby government to address issues of inequity and injustice. Not that evangelicals will consistently agree on the steps that should be taken – for example, in regard to issues of military intervention in countries – but it is about developing an awareness within congregations and communities that global issues are local issues and local issues can have global implications, and that if Christians are to take seriously the rule of love your neighbour as yourself, there has never been a time in the history of the planet or the history of this country where that neighbour is more likely to be of a different ethnicity, culture, religion or background. This is an opportunity – a wonderful chance to make multicultural, multifaith spaces that are genuinely beloved communities. The survey responses hint that this is a desire on the part of some, but also hints at a possible narrowing of attitudes and a desire to have global connections but within a national identity framework.

I think one of the key responsibilities of the church 'going' is to champion the global nature of its community, to forge ever closer links with neighbours local, national and global, and through its influence and its practices to provide spaces and open up avenues for multicultural, multilayered beloved communities to develop and flourish.

References

Castles, Stephen; De Haas, Hein; Miller, Mark J. (2013, fifth edition). *The Age of Migration: International Population Movements in the Modern World*. New York: Palgrave Macmillan.

Chaplain, Jonathan (2011). *Multiculturalism*: A Christian Retrieval. London, Theos.

Jenkins, Philip (2007). *The Next Christendom: The Coming of Global Christianity*. Oxford: Oxford University Press.

McGrath, Alister (2007). *Christianity's Dangerous Idea: The Protestant Revolution – a history from the sixteenth century to the twenty-first* (New York: HarperCollins Publishers.

Reddie, Richard S. (2007). *Abolition! The Struggle to Abolish Slavery in the British Colonies*, Oxford: Lion Hudson.

Sanneh, Lamin (2008) Disciples of All Nations Pillars of World Christianity. Oxford: Oxford University Press.

Solomos, John (2003, third edition). *Race and Racism in Britain*. Basingstoke: Palgrave Macmillan.

Response to chapter 8
Rev Israel Oluwole Olofinjana

Here I am meant to give a short response to Dr Ackah's insightful perspective on the global nature of evangelicalism and how it is adapting to the dynamics of global and transnational processes. The surveys with which this chapter engages consider different attitudes and adjustments of British evangelicals to issues of immigration, global poverty, interfaith engagement, social justice, the persecuted church, nationalism, cultural diversity and war. While the survey data reveals that overall, evangelical Christians are adapting well to the dynamics of globalisation and transnationalism and the impact they have had on Britain, there is still a sense of difference between minority and majority ethnic experience, and that evangelicals 'do work' in minority communities as opposed to being an integral part of those communities. In addition, the data suggests that although British evangelicals place a high value on their Christian identity and have in many cases engaged in missionary activity abroad, the depth of that identification and engagement at home, with either one's neighbour or one's community, is not deep enough.

How can our engagement abroad, either through aid relief or as a former missionary, translate into concrete action at home? This will necessitate a new thinking and intentionality. We certainly have to engage in dialogue and listening to our brothers and sisters from other faiths living in the UK, and learn about other cultures by talking to people in our community whose ethnicity is different from our own. Building strategic relationships and intentional partnering is essential for home missions. One way to proceed might be to partner with an Indian church, for example, so as to understand the Indian culture in all its diversity of religion and ethnicity.

It is good to read that 74% of people think we need missionaries from other countries to bring the gospel to the UK. This is in recognition that Britain is now a mission field and that the representative Christianity in the twenty-first century is no longer Europe or the United States, but Latin America, Asia and Africa. As someone who came to these shores as a missionary a decade ago and is ministering in multi-ethnic and multicultural congregations, I serve as an example of the reverse flow of mission. However, I am equally aware of the need for partnership between those from the majority world and the indigenous British so as to bring about God's kingdom in this part of the world.

The issue of partnership is one that the Evangelical Alliance is pursuing through the initiative of the One People Commission, with its vision of unity in diversity. This initiative brings together national and denominational leaders of black majority churches, Asian churches, Chinese churches and, more recently, Latin American churches. While this is a national initiative, it is important for church leaders to build local partnerships through local ecumenical instruments or through building relationship with pastors from different ethnic backgrounds.

The multi-ethnic partnership developed by the Evangelical Alliance is reflective of evangelical Christianity as a global movement from the eighteenth and nineteenth centuries, with its transatlantic movement with leaders such as Whitefield ministering in the States and Wesley in Britain.

Rev Israel Oluwole Olofinjana is the pastor at Woolwich Central Baptist Church.

Concluding remarks: A cause for hope

Dave Landrum

The *21st Century Evangelicals* research offers some fascinating and unique insights about evangelical Christians in the UK today. We can be grateful that such a group of expert social scientists who understand the dimensions of contemporary culture and religion have come together to produce this volume for us. In general, they present a positive picture of health and vitality. Yet the authors also identify some significant challenges for today's church.

Steve Holmes' first chapter on evangelical identity helpfully sets the scene by focusing on two important issues facing the growing evangelical church today: theological challenges and cultural challenges. Evangelicalism has long been defined by a desire for clarity about theological and doctrinal boundaries and, as Steve points out, the research confirms how these are accompanied by discernibly sociological phenomena. Even so, despite all the social capital that evangelicals bring to public life, we can also see a social context marked by public apathy and secularist agendas. Much of this helps to fuel negative stereotypes in our largely religiously illiterate and occasionally hostile media which sometimes likes to depict evangelicals as reactionary, bigoted, political conservatives – something that the *21st Century Evangelicals* research helps to dispel.

Despite the challenges, the book shows that the evangelical label has great value, and the good news it conveys is worth fighting for. As Steve Holmes observes, the apparent solidity of evangelical identity in the face of so many challenges and social complexities can be seen as an encouraging sign of a church that values its history and theology. Furthermore, the range and scope of evangelical activity highlighted by the research may help explain why the label attracts both praise and criticism within society.

Within the church, the push and pull around evangelical identity seems to largely accord with the comfort or discomfort that relates to evangelism – the core thing that sets an evangelical apart from other Christians. When both walking (behaviour) and talking (proclamation) the gospel seem to be at odds with our increasingly liberal authoritarian culture, it is easy to see how evangelical identity can either dissolve or harden.

Alongside this, there is clearly an agenda by some who self-identify as evangelicals but could more accurately be described as liberal Protestants seeking to lay claim to the word 'evangelical'. Whether this is for ideological reasons or simply to tap into the 'market' for financial gain via book sales, the result is that those most sympathetic to such perspectives are often simply enculturated to secularism through fear or fashion.

At the other end of the spectrum, and partly as a reaction to this secularisation of the soul, an identity can form in which moralism fuels a discourse of defensive decline. This 'shouting at the world' identity owes more to Christendom and modernity than to the New Testament, and represents a form of enculturation by failure and frustration.

Clearly, neither of these poles of identity resemble the hopeful, confident and dynamic evangelicalism of our illustrious forebears – nor do they seem to have a future beyond either cultural capitulation or culture warring.

Where there is clarity and authority on 'life and doctrine' within a loving community, there is life. This can be seen in the analysis of research on church life by Mandy Robbins and Greg Smith which confirms much of what we already knew – that many evangelical churches are thriving and growing. Indeed, they are highly valued as places of learning, fellowship and support by most of their members. In an age of individualism and indifference, this devotion to the life of the gathered community of God's people is encouragingly countercultural. Alongside the need to maintain momentum through a focus on conversion growth, there is also a challenge for evangelicals to provide a working model of a truly plural society to a world that is struggling to reconcile equality with diversity. Here the church can go beyond providing a context for each member to fulfil their own God-given destiny to providing a context for whole communities to fulfil their God-given destinies – becoming a collective foretaste of or witness to a new creation, where everyone has a role to play and is loved.

Greg Smith's chapter on social involvement underlines the point that evangelicals are natural activists. Indeed, the research shows how those with strong orthodox beliefs and moral values are far more likely than average to be involved in serving their communities and to be involved in voluntary projects. As active citizens and good neighbours, in relation to social (and spiritual) capital, the associational value that these evangelicals bring to civil society is significant. Indeed, in an age of welfare reform and austerity it is clear that social service provision in many districts would fall apart without the contribution of the churches and their members. As local authorities are subjected to increasing capacity demands and financial restrictions in the years ahead, there will be a challenge for Christians to go further.

With local communities requiring more effective, grass-roots public leadership, there is a responsibility for churches to up their game and develop appropriate ways of working in partnership with secular agencies. They will need to do this without compromising their convictions on important issues, insisting on the freedom to speak up about their faith. Alongside needing to develop more professional approaches, better language for engagement and confidence to operate beyond the 'Christian cocoon' will be the need to sometimes be a prophetic voice, speaking truth to power and questioning unjust polices – and all in an environment where secular assumptions and religious illiteracy predominate. So, despite the higher levels of social activism, it seems that as many challenges as opportunities lie ahead.

Politics has always been important to evangelicals, and Matthew Guest's chapter on politics shows that this is continuing today. He identifies a readiness to engage in political action, such as volunteering and campaigning, that sets evangelicals apart from the apathy of broader society. We may well be doing politics in an anti-political age and within a political culture that is dominated by elites who 'don't do God', but even so, evangelicals are more likely to vote, and there is clearly a strong public service ethic in the church. And this engagement is not monolithic. Matthew shows a diverse range of domestic and international issues that compel evangelicals to political action, such as poverty, freedom, social inequality, abortion and overseas development.

In terms of party support, evangelicals also seem to be diverse, although a recent marked drop in Conservative and an accompanying spike in UKIP support is notable. This shift is shown to be overwhelmingly related to the government's redefinition of marriage. As an augmentation to the pre-existing positions on Europe and immigration, it could be said to be the issue that effectively boosted the UKIP vote to its present heady heights. Illustrative of the disconnection between largely secularised, liberal, political elites and religious people with traditional moral views, the research suggests that the three main parties face major challenges to win support from disillusioned evangelicals. Furthermore, given that generally evangelicals seem to be 'conservative on issues of theology and sexual ethics, while fairly left-leaning in their politics', it seems that the standard political bipolarity of left and right is now insufficient as a descriptor for this growing and active constituency.

All of this points to the need for evangelicals to resist the indifference that characterises many in the UK who see politics as broken. Hopefully, with such an active predisposition, evangelicals will increasingly see themselves as part of the solution to the present staleness of social and economic liberalism. Drawing inspiration from an illustrious history of political leadership, if evangelicals can once again see politics in missional terms, they can play an important role in the post-liberal future that is drawing closer.

Sylvia Collins-Mayo's excellent chapter picks up the theme of gender in the evangelical community. Tracing the impact of social change on women's lives, she concludes that even in a context of major disagreements in the church over gender roles, evangelical women's lives and expectations are not that different from their non-Christian counterparts.

Keith White's chapter shows that the majority of Christians remain strongly committed to traditional forms of marriage and the family and as such can be seen to stand apart from the new social orthodoxy that was recently enacted through the government's redefinition of marriage. Evangelical resistance to such cultural pressure is an encouraging expression of countercultural witness, as is the commitment to running marriage courses. However, the research shows that more needs to be done by churches to support single people (particularly women), and also to develop more accessible pastoral support for those struggling with relationship issues.

In relation to fatherhood, there is clearly a strong valuing of male role models within families. Yet, amid a range of views on family roles, there is also a recognition that the economic demands of our consumer society are having a detrimental effect upon family time and relational bonds. Here, evangelicals see the extended family as an important resource. However, in light of the clearly stated valuing of family by evangelicals, and given the increasing neo-liberal economic and cultural pressures upon the integrity of family life, it could be said that the broader church community has a responsibility to play a more intentional role in providing practical support for working families. Indeed, in relation to the nurture of children and the transmission of faith through prayer and Bible study, Keith's analysis identifies the family as 'little church', but suggests that the overlapping and mutually supporting roles of the family and the church may be undervalued. He observes that our social situation 'demands a corporate response' and that 'it may well take a village to raise children in the Christian faith in future'. Alongside this, in terms of scheduled church activities, it is concerning that there seems to be such a comparatively small outward focus on 'non-churched' children and young people. As we seek to address the challenge of a 'missing generation' in church life, surely evangelistic children's ministry and youth outreach need to become priorities?

Among evangelical parents and carers there is a high level of awareness about the ongoing sensory bombardment of family life and relationships with antithetical secular values. This is accompanied by a holistic view of the purpose of education and a desire to see an education system that is primarily informed by Christianity. These views indicate that there is a need for churches and other organisations to more adequately 'equip children and young people with the Christian resources to withstand the pervading secular atheism'. This equipping of young people to identify and counter the pressures of secularism is an urgent priority for the church today.

Even so, although the research shows that despite evangelical women sharing many of the same views as evangelical men, they experience similar levels of discrimination in church as they do in society. For a church that has been at the historical vanguard of women's rights and equality (while celebrating diversity between the sexes), Sylvia's analysis reveals a persistence of too many cases of disadvantage, and sometimes abuse. Her statement is striking that, in terms of the 'different but equal' maxim, 'we're not there yet!' This is a prescient observation considering that women are the numerical majority in the UK church. Their disproportionate lack of influence and authority presents some thorny issues for a church in which there is a range of theological views on gender roles. Although this disproportionality will no doubt be hard to resolve, it is clear that women have an increasingly important and prominent role to play in the life of the growing evangelical church in the UK. Indeed, a church that is full of strong men and strong women would not only be a countercultural witness to the faux equality of secular society; it would also greatly benefit the mission of the gospel.

The review by William Kay and Mandy Robbins on the charismatic movement within the evangelical community provides a fascinating framework for understanding the nature of belief and practice in the church today. Identifying features such as high church attendance, a strong relational focus and a distinction between church as people rather than buildings, this stream is seen as confident and outward looking. Although the research shows that the charismatic church is largely middle class in the UK, it is clear that social changes are afoot with the recent growth of Pentecostal immigrant and ethnic minority church networks. Interestingly (perhaps encouragingly?), there are natural affinities between charismatics and traditional evangelical groups on the frequency and focus of prayer.

This chapter gives an insight into an important part of the church in the UK, and is a helpful resource for better understanding the theological, social, political, economic and cultural impact of this growing stream of the evangelical community. Identifying many points of convergence with other evangelical streams on issues of morality and social justice, the analysis also highlights the distinctive features of a dynamic, generous and confident charismatic church in the UK. All of this suggests that the contemporary relevance of the work of the Holy Spirit is now more widely accepted. In terms of the gospel, this bodes well for the future. It also places the primary unifying role of the Evangelical Alliance as an important element of God's mission in the UK.

The final chapter by William Ackah shows how evangelicalism continues to be true to its ethos as a global religious movement. It also shows how this movement is changing as a result of globalisation and transnationalism, and is set to have a profound political, economic and cultural impact in the years ahead.

While the respondents to our survey are overwhelmingly white British in background, it is encouraging that they are aware and generally welcoming of Christians from other communities. The analysis also reassuringly shows that UK evangelicals remain strongly committed to global evangelisation, with many individuals and churches maintaining significant relationships with a variety of missional activities overseas. As the UK church increasingly benefits from the influx of the migrant church, it is heartening that there is a broad appreciation for the process of 'reverse mission' as a timely, returning blessing. This is reflected in the Evangelical Alliance's creation of the One People Commission which exists to better include and reflect the ethnic diversity of the UK church.

Fascinatingly, in relation to this distinctive and developing global outlook, the data may even suggest that there is a general welcoming shift in the gravitational centre of the global church away from the North and the West towards the East and the South. In our climate of economic 'progress' and transnational competition, this is countercultural *in extremis*. In connection with this attitude, evangelicals also continue to be at the forefront of Christian action to tackle world poverty and injustice, with the analysis showing an equal emphasis on domestic and international giving.

Ackah identifies very high support for the persecuted church, which is encouraging for the developing work of the Evangelical Alliance's newly formed Religious Liberty Commission (which includes Open Doors, Christian Solidarity Worldwide and Release International). This unified voice is committed to seeing the church play its role in prayerfully and practically supporting brothers and sisters across the world who are suffering for their faith in Jesus. Impressively, evangelicals cite their identity as followers of Christ above all other claims on identity such as class, race, gender, nation, region and ethnicity. This helps explain why, in a political climate that is often characterised by hostility towards immigration, they are also accepting of the idea of mission in reverse and of learning from the faith and vibrancy of Christians in other parts of the world. Indeed, this unity of the Spirit with whole body of Christ across the world may well be obvious, but in our ever fragmenting world, it should be more openly celebrated as a witness to our culture. It is a remarkable statement of faithfulness to the command of Jesus to love one another, and provides a model for a society that is struggling to find ways to live with differences.

The Alliance clearly has a role to play to practically maintain unity with the broader evangelical church across the globe. In relation to the keen interest in the persecuted church, the work of the Religious Liberty Commission will be vital for raising prayer and public consciousness in the years ahead. With the global analysis showing an equal emphasis on domestic and international giving, yet a lack of knowledge about policy specifics related to campaigning, there is clearly a responsibility for the Alliance to provide more political information.

Significantly, as the representative voice for the two million evangelicals in the UK – a constituency that the research shows is increasingly ethnically diverse – the Alliance has a responsibility to represent diversity in a culturally sensitive and proportionate way. Here, the work of our One People Commission will be vital for the future unity of the church and the gospel in the UK. And if the early signs of friendship and fellowship are anything to go by, then our future is bright indeed.

Furthermore, as cross-cultural mission continues to become a priority in the UK, there is also a role for the Alliance to provide theological resources for evangelicals to be able to engage with other faith groups, both missionally in terms of proclaiming the gospel for salvation and strategically in terms of working together to secure religious freedom and to enhance faith relations in a plural society.

The analysis in this book is drawn from a research programme that covers a vast range of themes and issues that are important to evangelicals. It shows how cultural pressures to conform and acquiesce to secular ideals are being resisted and confronted, and it identifies the challenges and opportunities that lie ahead for this growing and vibrant part of the church.

The Evangelical Alliance hopes that this book will provide a valuable resource for the church to be effective and distinctive in its mission of proclaiming and demonstrating the gospel for the salvation of souls. This is what is at the heart of evangelicalism – a gospel obsession that sets us apart from other forms of Christianity – a compulsion to reach out, to serve and to love the lost. This also means that for evangelicals there is a strong connection between life (how we live) and doctrine (what we believe). Evangelism that is an effective and faithful witness to the gospel must involve both. Taken together, the analysis contained in this book suggests that evangelicals will continue to be fruitful witnesses individually and collectively to the degree that they take seriously Paul's injunction to 'Watch your life and doctrine closely. Persevere in them, because if you do, you will save both yourself and your hearers.' (1 Timothy 4:16). I'm encouraged that, despite the challenges of the church and the culture, evangelicals are endeavouring to do this.

References

Christians in Parliament, 'Faith in the Community – strengthening ties between faith groups and local authorities' (June 2013) produced by Evangelical Alliance. Available at http://www.eauk.org/current-affairs/publications/loader.cfm?csModule=security/getfile&pageid=38452 (accessed 18th December 2014).